The Tears
I Cried,
He Dried

Eileen O'Driscoll

ORIGINAL WRITING

978-1-907179-74-7

A CIP catalogue for this book is available from the National Library.

Published by Original Writing Ltd., Dublin, 2010.

Printed by Cahill Printers Limited, Dublin.

Dedication

In memory of my dear husband Brian.

To my family;

Brian Og, Lucy, Fiona, Nollaig and John.

ACKNOWLEDGEMENT

To write this book, I give my family the greatest acknowledgement,Writing it has healed my inner child, and my fears are demolished,My faith with God, is enduring and polished.

For my children's support, I say a big 'Thank You' Because with them, I would never have carried through, I now know my true connection, and to God I give appreciation.I hope others, too, will be healed through prayer and mediation, I give a sincere ' Thank You' to my friends, who gave me inspiration, And for their prayers of praise and adoration. Without everyone who was totally involved, The puzzle of my life would never have been solved. I give the greatest 'Thank You' of all to my Holy Father, For opening my eyes, so I could see Him broader.

I have grown to love Him as I now see how he carried me day by day,In my book, His guidance has led the way.I truly hope my book will give others a true conversion,And that they too can learn, that they are a worthwhile person, Everyone can be healed with the right direction, Reading this book, you will see God's true love and affection. This is a story of how Jesus healed me of my brokeness and is now using me as a tool to heal others.

I would like to thank Anne for all her help, support and all her endless patience I would like to thank Vicky for her work in producing the final version. I would also like to thank my daughter Fiona for supporting me and encouraging me to write this book.

I would also like to thank all the people who gave me permission to write their testimonies of how Jesus healed them.

v

The Highlights of my Story

The Waters were Deep but with the Lord I did keep

I take a breather, and just as I relax,
I decide to write my autobiography of all the years gone back,
From the moment I can remember to the very present.
This book will be a glimpse of one
Born into a family of despair,
To be tormented by a mother layer by layer,
Suffering at her hands that were so cruel.
To my Mother I was a fool,
But not alone at the hands of Mother was I abused,
By the emotional trauma I was confused,
And behind closed doors by other people I was affected.
I was like a worm, I was dissected.
With physical, mental and all kinds of scarring
From treatment so cruel, I was like the road that was tarring.
Mother, knowing that I was the victim of evil perpetrators,
Turned a blind eye to their capers.
I had wounds so deep I felt nobody cared,
I was the victim of torture, the burdens of it I had to bear.
My Father to me was like a touch of heaven,
To be out of Mother's sight with him I would count up to seven,
Wherever she went she made me follow too,
She was my infection, just like the flu.
My sisters were the part; I was the outcast,
And judging by them was done very fast.
To my family I was like Cinderella,
To protect Mother for her evilness I was made the umbrella.
Time passed very quickly and I soon grew up
To taste the goodness outside Mother, sip by sip,
The chains were broken one by one and I became free,
My life now started to be controlled by me.
I met a man, if I may so call him, a gentleman,
With him my life really began.

He thought to love me was not a crime,
And he became my husband, his name was Brian.
With Him a new life I explored,
A new sense of peace, hope and love poured,
My life was happy and started sailing.
I had to settle in the country but the isolation caused my failing,
I could not stand to be alone,
The strain of the countryside caused me to moan,
I missed people and it gave me depression,
I felt it was Mother again trying to teach me a lesson.
I had five children, who made my heart smile,
And for their sake I wore a mask made of foil.
Our love for them had no end,
They were my joy, happiness and strength,
And my life I gave to them at length.
They were my flowers that grew into towers,
They were my friends that the Lord had sent,
The world to me they meant,
Without them nowhere I went.
My suffering in life didn't end just there,
My third child suffered too, life wasn't fair.
At the hands of doctors and nuns,
The piercing of our hearts was no fun,
Lies, deceit, whatever you want to call it,
With a bomb my life was hit.
Through prayers and petitions my child became normal
And that was the Lord's will.
She is now my strength and guide,
And my secrets in her I can confide.
I began to use Divine knowledge,
In starting a guesthouse, meeting people, I felt I was back in college,
Life improved but only for a few years,
For the rest I shed many tears.
My children were happy as they did prosper,
And like me, God they fostered,
What a joy it is to a mother to see her children cheerful,
Jesus gave them strength, like me, to pull,

And time rolled on and my children are now adults.
My husband became unwell and because of it life was dull,
My suffering was severe, at times I felt I had no pulse,
It seemed his awful sickness was a curse.
Worn out, I did the work of three men,
But wearing out my body like this was a sin.
On a sunny day I decided I would like a change,
And get out of the life I was living, which was very strange.
I bought a house, which was full of peace,
And it was the first time in my life that I felt my happiness increase,
It was a house that was specially chosen by God,
So I could do His plan, guided by the Lord.
My husband passed away and I am now a widow,
But since I came to this house my life is nothing but go.
The garden, which has Divine inspiration,
Has Him as the controller, and He is the Mason.
I am very happy now, I have the Lord's will to the brim,
Jesus has given me my fill.
Part of the learning was to forgive,
Until then my life I could not live.
Through suffering God turns our lives around,
And in Him a profound faith I have found.
I am His tool; I can do His work and give Him praise,
And likewise into your heart too He can blaze,
And from the hellhole give you a raise,
Happiness, hope and peace will be the menu on the trays.
This is the book of one who was lost,
And part of the learning came at a cost.
Life is a journey which we all lead,
But if we pray to the Lord to guide us He will help us indeed.
No man can step so low he cannot be helped,
Because God's armour is buckled around you like a belt.
The truth of God has set me free,
And the story of my life I tell you with glee,
About the change He made to me.
Remember nothing is impossible
As it says in the gospel.

INTRODUCTION

This book is my autobiography. It is the story of how once I was trapped as a child, in my own body. I was not allowed to explore or play and my development was impaired. Play is so important and it is part of a child's life. Through play you learn to express your emotions: love, joy, laughter, sorrow, pain and anger. My impairment was owing to my Mother. She kept me down, causing me horrendous fear. I was always alone and my sisters were looked up to like gods. I was always full of envy. I had so much mistrust towards my mother and trusting is very important as it gives us a sense of security. A child needs to feel secure in order to be able to play and, if there is no security, the child will feel uncomfortable and not play freely. I never thought like other children because I had more important things to deal with, like when the next beating was going to be and how I was going to avoid it.

In my life I was always living on the edge. Things could have gone either way, because I didn't know what she'd come up with next and that fear is still in the child inside me, today. Although I am being healed, healing can take many years. The good news is that I found Jesus in time. He was always there, but I could not focus on Him, as there was too many obstacles in the way.

When I did meet Him it was as if He wrapped His arms around me and I could hear the words in my heart, ' you're going to get over this and I am holding you up. You will not suffer because I will be your Father, Mother, Brother and sister or whatever you want me to be, and that is the way it has been since. I've never let go of the hand of God; there is still baggage that needs to be sorted, but He has brought me this far. It is many years since all this suffering began, but I was trapped because I was still not able to express how I felt. It seemed to me that I was not a normal person in society. I am a person now that has been re-moulded. I have new ideas, new thoughts and new interests and I think positively.

God is now using me to help people who had a life like me. About 12 years ago, God gave me a wonderful gift of healing and I have been using this gift successfully ever since for people with cancer, heart defects, depression and countless other illnesses.

What a privilege it is to do God's work. I am honoured to be His servant. About 3 years ago, I turned my beautiful rose garden into a prayer garden called 'A Moment with Jesus and Mary'. Lots of broken people come and find peace and an answer to their problems.

With my third child I also suffered an awful lot and as an adult this has brought me into deeper prayer. My third child was healed of autism through the intercession of Little Nellie, the Cork saint. My daughter is a very happy, healthy, young woman today and, like me, God has given her wonderful gifts and all the fruits of the Holy Spirit. She helps me with the garden and is a great support to me.

Throughout this book there are many stories and testimonies of other people and how they were healed. My life is summed up in zigzag lines, because it has gone from one extreme to the other. There have been joyful stories too, because through Jesus you learn to have joy and you learn to laugh, and when you put your hope in Jesus you will be as solid as a rock.

After every dark night there will be light, for suffering does not last forever. Jesus will give you back the years the locusts have taken away. You will think differently, and attitude is more important than facts. It's the way you look at something that causes the problem. 'With Joy, draw water from the well of salvation' Isiah 4-5. Jesus will hold you upright with his hands and do not let any one make you crumble as God is better than any man is. Jesus is the same yesterday, today and forever and what He has done for me He can do for you. He has conquered my life and He is now waiting to conquer yours.

THE TRANQUILISING LORD

My name is Eileen Theresa O`Driscoll and this is the story of my life. The Lord opened a gate of happiness in 1990, when my children, Brian, and myself, moved to town. I am happier living in this house than I have ever been in my life.

Here I am, sitting by a lovely cosy fire. My husband Brian always used to say that, `a good, cheerful, coal fire is very welcoming when you enter a room. It is nicer to look at than the most expensive furniture`. On the mantle piece over the fireplace is a candle. Three quarters of it has melted away. I have reached that stage in my own life as a senior citizen at the age of 66, and as I relax have decided to write my story. This is the story of my life.

I had a hard, cruel childhood and a great deal of suffering in my life and I am writing this book for two reasons. The first is to heal myself of painful memories and the second is to help others who have gone through a lot of pain in their childhood by explaining how I was healed. Sometimes I look out of the window and up at the sky and I see black and white clouds, and the sun peeping through this reminds me of own life. They are the black shadows and the light of Jesus is trying to penetrate them. ' The Lord is my light and my salvation whom shall I fear' Psalm 27. I was lucky I found God early on in life, but He is still healing me of my hardened childhood wounds. The scars are being lifted, layer by layer, in the ocean of His Divine Mercy. For some reason I held on to these wounds and secret memories. I was afraid to let go. It was as if they were mine and nobody was going to invade that part of me.

I was born into a family of four girls. The nursing home I was born into was run by a Miss Beamish and is now an old folk's centre. When I pass it, I sometimes think about how my life began. I feel my mother never wanted me before I was born. She told me at one time, that she was ill carrying me. Some of my mother's cruelty I can remember, more of it I can't, as I learned from a very young age to block off the painful memories. But they still haunt me, especially when making decisions, and I still suffer today from low self-esteem.

When a child is born, what grace it brings. Looking at it would make you smile and a smiling baby itself, has such a tranquilising effect. I wish it could have been like that for my mother, when I came into the world. I feel that I must have been an unwanted child, from the way that I was brought up. Something welled up inside me, even when a very young child, that gave me the eerie feeling my mother wanted to abandon me.

I grew up on a farm. My mother had great faith, and Mass and the sacraments were a big part of her life. I was very close to my Father and he was the one man who never caused me any hurt. He was a wonderful father and had a great sense of humour. My aunt Pet lived with us. She suffered from seizures all her life, as a result of the meningitis that she had as a child. There were no antibiotics in those days to treat her or bring down her high temperature. She showed me a lot of love as a child.

Life in the country was very hard in those days, because in the 1940's and early 1950's, rural Ireland had no electricity, no running water, no bathroom or no flush toilets. Pet worked hard in the farmyard feeding cattle and pigs, and milking cows. She had no social life; her only break was going to Mass on Sunday and chatting with neighbours on her way. As a result of her illness she had to go to a mental hospital periodically, but she never received any treatment for her illness. I do not know if she was ever brought to a doctor or not. Her suffering was intense and her seizures were like miniature strokes. Her body would become paralysed on one side and she would fall unconscious. Following these bouts she would become completely unaware of her surroundings for some hours. At times she would become aggressive. Her recovery period could take up to seven days but as soon as she came out of this state, it was right back to her heavy outdoor schedule on the farm. Nan also lived with us. She was my father's stepmother and she was very kind and motherly towards me, which I desperately needed at the time. She taught me my prayers. When I was 10 years old she died and I cried for days. I can still remember the pain of her passing.

I started school when I was 5 years old. I had to walk 2 miles to the little, stone-built, dark and dreary building. I took a bottle of milk and a sandwich with me. When we arrived, our milk bottles were put in front of an open fire, so that the milk would be warm at lunchtime. Our schoolteacher was very cross and wicked. She was a Miss Lynch and if we were five minutes late she would beat us with a big stick. She caned other children in the class for spelling mistakes or if they did not have their homework done to her satisfaction. She was very intolerant with children who were slow learners. When she beat other children I, being a sensitive child, could feel their pain. It upset me more than if she beat me. She had her pets, which were usually children from well-off families. I think she was afraid that the parents of these families might report her for cruelty. She was extra cruel to poor families, because in those days the poor in Ireland had no voice. We had to take firewood to school to keep us warm in the cold, bitter winter. Every day, especially on my way to school, I prayed to Jesus that Miss Lynch would die. When I arrived in school and found her still alive - wearing the white blouse, red cardigan and black skirt, which she wore every day - I thought Jesus did not hear my prayers. My Father told her off on one occasion and she mellowed for a short while.

When I was a child I suffered terribly from fear. It affected me in later life, especially at work. I was never able to stand up for myself and let everyone walk over me. I was afraid of relationships with men and I thought, perhaps it was because I had no brother? I had always longed for a brother. No young boys ever visited our house while I was growing up. I went to a `girls only ` boarding school and I thought this was another reason for my fear of boys. When I met Brian I felt he was different; he was so gentle and kind and I could talk to him freely. I always had a fear of sex and I could never understand why. I suffered intense fear coming up to my marriage. Jesus said ' let

not your heart be troubled. Trust in God and trust also in me'
'John 14.

In later life it was revealed to me that I was sexually abused
as a very young child. This suddenly explained my fear. I had
felt the fear, but I had not known the cause.

On many days I walked alone, thinking how things could be
different. Really, everything could not be my fault. Why did I
blame myself? A pack of wolves were at home, ready to devour
me, the chicken. In my glass there was no clean water, only grit.
I trained my mind only to think of good, otherwise I would
not have coped. I felt I had no one to turn to, except Father. I
had to walk my own plank and sometimes it was so wobbly I
thought I would fall.

Nowadays, when I go for a walk, my mind goes back down
memory lane. I think of the loneliness, the emptiness and the
fear that were all combined. There was no compassion, no
love and no peace, just a dreadful emptiness that would hold
you down. I had to fight every day for my survival.Because
of Mother, I had only one toy that I can remember. It was a
shabby teddy bear, fawn in colour and I called him Lala. When
you have few, or no, toys, you invent your own, because as the
saying goes, 'necessity is the mother of invention'. I used to get
long stones and cover them with moss and pretend they were
dolls and find bits of crockery and stick them into a hedge to
make my shop. Some of the broken crockery was in bright colours and I love bright colours to this day. I would just begin to
play when Mother called, because work was for me, not play.

For the first four years of my life my imagination was limited, because of the boundaries Mother had set. These boundaries affected my thought patterns. After so many dull incidents
in school and home life, I would imagine good things. If I was
in a shop I might see a mother giving her child a hug. I would
keep this image in my mind and every night I dreamt of this
mother hugging and kissing me. Some of these images could
last for years. I would crave for affection and even if someone
stroked my hand it gave me the fulfilment of being loved. I
would always try and be in other peoples company to get rid of

the loneliness. I would have so many dreams of beautiful things happening in my life but, when I awoke in the morning, it was back to sad reality.

I lived in a dream world and if I had not I would have been insane, as I could not have coped. My dreams were about change. After a dream I would imagine Mother had these qualities and I tried to believe she loved me, but I was always let down. I always dreamt of Nan being a mother to me. A smile from Nan seemed to last an eternity. In some of my dreams I thought I was dying, and that a lot of people were standing around my bed, asking me if I was O.K. I was under the illusion, that if I were dying I would get a lot of love and affection. Then the attention would be all on me. I believed that the only love I ever received was from the imaginary people in my dreams. The sense of touch, showed love to me. I knew my dreams were unrealistic but that was the only way my mind could cope, because you dream the way you feel.

Sometimes I would have nightmares because of Mother's treatment and would wake up in terror. I used the image of good to block out the bad but, if you have black paint on the wall and paint white over it, the black will still come out. It is like brushing the dirt under the carpet. My pain was still there. At times, when I saw an animal being stroked, the craving inside was like a knife piercing me. I thought I was abnormal because of all the weird dreams I had. I could never understand the strange things I imagined. It was my little world, like being in the cornfields. It was like a breath of fresh air and was the only way my mind could cope with the cruelty. In life I had nobody to talk to. I really believe that God was working in my unconscious mind, unknown by myself.

I had to work very hard, cleaning the house and working out in the fields. Water had to be drawn with a sweet gallon tin, which had a wire handle. Sometimes the handle would cut into my hands and my little fingers were sore. I had to get up very early in the morning to help cook the breakfast and when I got older I also had to milk the cows before I went to school. I remember that once Mother put me into a tub of very hot water and perhaps that is one reason why I have this terrible fear of water to this very day. Maybe she did it because I was dirty from the fields. I do not know. Another time, when I was about 4 years old, she got some insects and made them crawl over me. She thought this was fun. I was absolutely petrified and when I saw her laughing and the evil look in her eyes it left me very confused. The insects stung me and I was too frightened to cry. From then on, I tried to block off pain and also tears. Later on, I developed a way of coping with these traumatic events. I did not cry, or show emotion, because if I did she would do it all the more. One thing my Mother hated was anyone making a fuss, and if I did, I would hear about it, because she did not want anyone to know her wicked ways.

I still suffer from all kinds of fear but the Lord is gradually healing me. The scars are lifted, layer by layer, and the precious blood of God's gentle ocean is washing them away. I thank You and praise You, my uplifting father. ' The Lord is the stronghold of my life, of whom shall I be afraid. ' Psalm 27.

Everyone thought my Mother was a saint and to most people she was. Nobody knew what was happening behind closed doors. Never say that you know what is going on in someone else's life. To me, the outward spectacle is a myth. God had never forsaken me, but at times I felt He had. Now, years later, I realise He never abandoned me; I just did not understand His ways back then.

When my Mother told me I would never marry, I felt I was ugly and useless and as if life had no purpose or value. I felt as if I was just taking up a space on earth and I hated myself. Mother taught me not to love myself from a very young age. My emotions were suppressed and I worried about the future. I worried about whether I could ever love my husband or my children. Childhood is a foundation that we build on and I was always afraid I would turn out like Mother. Thank God I did not. My family always knew I loved them. God gave me the qualities that I should have got as a child. He embedded them into my life, even though I had no experience of them in childhood. God gave me greater abilities to do things than I could ever have imagined.

Even if you come from no class in society and are never taught to love, when you get to know God, He puts love into your heart because God is love. God cannot make a connection with man when there is no love. Love is the greatest force on earth; it will never hurt and helps everyone to be happy. Prayer is the greatest force for conversion to help us love. Prayer governs God and God governs the world with his everlasting love.

Following all the abuse I had as a child I never received counselling or any therapy to get me through. I relied totally on God. I was afraid to tell anyone else because I had the fear that I would not be believed. I did confront Mother in later life. She walked away, but I knew by her face that she was shocked when I asked. She knew that she could no longer fool me. Her days of covering up were over. A mother is meant to protect her child and she knew that was important. When I asked her about the abuse, it hit her that she had failed, not alone on the level of caring but also on my protection. Looking back I sometimes wonder if that was the reason that Mother could never get on with me. Perhaps I reminded her too much of what had happened, and as long as I was there she could never blot it out. Her inward anger was directed towards me. In everything I did she put me down. I think it was a reflection of herself that she could not face.

I have forgiven my Mother but I think that she could not forgive herself. This was the biggest drawback for her, because she had to live with it. She was heavily burdened all her life. She got used to the idea of my being abused and looked down on me as dirt. I was the victim but she treated me as the guilty one. In later life, when I decided to marry, she thought Brian was too good for me. She thought I was not worthy of ever getting married because of my history of abuse. I soon gave her my answer. I got married but she could never get used to the idea. They say, 'your mother is the greatest person you will ever know,' but to me she made me low and gave my life mighty blows

Mother's Way, I Had No Say

I was born in the year of 1938,
February was the month; the 18th was the date,
One of four, no brothers but sisters,
Having no brother was just like a blister,
A mother who had faith, but did not recognise grace,
I was her little servant in this case.
I was like a robot that you turn on with a battery,
Her right hand man, I was like her main artery,
Doing as I was told, never to do wrong,
Inside I had to be very strong.
But now my life is a story that is miraculous,
I have found my place on the atlas,
A place with God where I will never look back,
With Him I have everything, nothing do I lack

May His Hands Hold Me
and His Feet Carry me

Lord Jesus, hold my hand wherever I go, walk me back into my fears of my childhood. Walk me through the darkness so, with You no evil shall I fear. Help me to conquer all and overcome my fears so these fears do not take control of my life today. Help me come face to face with those people that caused me fear. Remove the hatred from my heart, Lord, that caused me to be bitter with these people. As I walk, Lord, I can feel the darkness and the emptiness of my childhood. With Your love, Lord, pour Your precious blood over my wounds and set me free from this darkness. Lord, as I hold Your hand, let it bond like glue to me, so I will never let go of Your hand again. Let these hands hold me and Your feet carry me through the darkness and the light. May every step I take be a reminder of Your love for me. Amen

ALONE AND UNPROTECTED

My Mother went to town, shopping, on Saturdays, and also regularly visited friends and relatives. When she left the house, she gave me over to the care of workmen, who were employed on our farm. My babysitters were always men. Some of them I do not remember, and some of them I do. They spoke openly to one another in the local public house about their abuse of me. Some of them treated it as a joke. But others denied it in later life. I feel they must have been guilty and disgusted by their acts, as by now they had become parents themselves.

To my horror, I discovered that some of my abuse took place when I was only eleven months old and finished when I was around 5 years old. Most of what took place I was too young to remember, although I did feel the terrible after-effects of fear and self-hatred. But I can remember the men beating me and abusing me both sexually and physically and the terror I felt when my mother left me in the care of these men.

Terence, a close relative on my mother's side of the family, was a regular visitor to the farm and I was informed in later life that he was the most frequent abuser – and abused me in a very severe way. Nowadays he would get a very long jail sentence. I have a feeling, gained from some of the feedback I heard in later life, that I might have been abused a few times in the one day, as the men boasted openly together about their evil deeds.

My Mother knew about the abuse and turned a blind eye to it. I do not know why my Mother did not protect me. It took place in her house and it was revealed to me that my Mother's relative informed her about his treatment of me – making light of the fact. My Mother would never discuss the issue in later life, although I brought it up. Perhaps my Mother was unable to deal with the subject, especially when it was done by such a close relative of hers and incestuous; she did not want to expose him. I have no explanation as to why my Mother did not act in my defence. It is very important to protect children who are at risk from paedophiles. It seemed as if Mother had control over me but was not concerned for my well being. I felt like the food given to the dogs and, no matter who treated me badly, nothing was said. The perpetrators were very strange because they knew when to pull the trigger. As you know every abuser is cunning, clever and cautious, and knows the moment to strike. When they were given such open freedom in my home they took the golden opportunity to abuse me. If a Mother does not protect her child, obviously there will be consequences in life. Some of them are fatal. That is the way it was for me. You cannot hand your child over to just anyone; just because they are a relative does not mean they will be nice.

Going back in years, incest was very common, but was never spoken about. Once it was found out, another relative took part in the crime. It was like an addiction. I think that was the weird edging on my abuse. It was like pass the parcel. I was the parcel and they were the receivers. All my life I knew that the abuse had an effect on my personality. It made me feel like scum, a lowlife and the dirt of the ground. I was not worthy of anything except to be treated like dirt.

Everyone goes through a grieving process when something happens to him. DID I GRIEVE? 'HA!' No, my feelings were locked inside and inside they stayed. I was like a zombie, not knowing how to express my true colours. An even better description is that I was like a scarecrow, a human being only on the outside. Inside I was dead.

Mother had to take me to the doctor, when I was 4 years old, and I remember her treating me with ointment every night. It was grey in colour and she put it on with a large spatula. One day, I confronted her, wondering why I was always sore, and she said harshly, "You fell down the stairs and hurt yourself". For years afterwards I felt sore, so much so that my Mother treated me every night with different powders. The wall of my womb was so damaged that I have suffered all my life, during my pregnancies and to this very day, with womb trouble. I was hospitalised at the age of nine years old for two weeks because my bowel was also damaged. It was revealed to me recently in prayer that I received the most severe molesting of all time.

So, life was very hard for me between 1 and 5 years old and these are very important years in a child's life. I was totally dependent on my Mother and I was completely defenceless because I was not developed. Whatever happened to me, I had to take it. When I reached the age of reason, I became aware of what was happening to me and had the ability to understand it, my mother did not allow it to happen anymore. But by that stage, the abuse had taken control of my life, along with the suffering my mother caused me with beatings.

WHEN I WAS A CHILD

When I was ten-years-old I went for a stroll down to the well field. The well field was very familiar to me because at that time we had no running water or toilet facilities in the house and I had to draw water every day. I also fed the chickens and the ducks in the haggard leading to the well field. I loved the noise of fowl, I felt they were speaking a language which no one could understand only themselves. I always got great pleasure listening to them and they were great company to me as I was a very lonely child.

When I was alone I could speak to God because of the suffering I endured. I asked Him to help me cope for another day. I suppose I was always close to God because of my childhood. I lost faith in God when I was seven years old as my life at that stage seem to fall in on top of me. I could not bear any more of Mother and her cruel ways. I realised at that age that I was abused and mentally tortured. I felt unable to cope any longer. Mother caused me to have a giant inferiority complex which had the effect of isolating me from people.

I never felt I had friends as a child. There were times I thought I would go insane. I at this stage not only suffered from loneliness but from depression. I was forever sad. Older people think children never get depressed. I wanted to run away. But I was never brave enough to do so. I made several attempts. I would run the distance of a couple of fields. Then I would get frightened and come back home. The problem really was I had no place to run to. I was stuck. It was the thought of freedom that made me run. I felt free in my spirit if only for a few minutes. The sensation I experienced must have felt like a drowning man coming up for air. I breathed freely if only for a short period of time. For that brief space of time – I lived. The rest was sheer survival.

What should have been normal for me I never knew, and looking at other children made me feel very unhappy. I would see Mothers collecting their children from school and thought that this was so special. To me they were children who were very well looked after.

When you are down in yourself, you become vulnerable. Other people sense this and manipulate your lack of confidence. I was a timid child and one teacher reacted by picking on me. Other children taunted me. It is funny how even a child can sense you are weak and play on your emotions. Even babies can learn how to manipulate parents. I had a want, a great desire inside, for an ideal person, who I wanted to love me.

I searched in the deep waters of my spirit, for this special person. But nobody could match my criteria. I persistently had a dream; a dream of a mother who would give her child hugs and kisses. I dreamt of me as a, child holding hands with a loving mother, and being shown affection from her in front of other people. It was somehow important to me that in public I would be seen as having someone near me who loved me and wanted me.

I found it hard to adapt at school. For a small child I had a lot on my mind and I was not like other children, thinking of the next toy. I was thinking of when I would get the next telling off. Other children did not know my suffering. , How could they understand? I was full of pain, bitterness and fear. Children would sometimes ask me to join in their games. Physically I would be there, but never in my mind. Because of what I suffered at home I lost a large portion of my childhood. I had burdens to carry and when I had the opportunities, like other children, to be happy, I could never be at peace, because my peace was violated by my troubles. People would smile at me and the next question I would ask myself was what was there to smile about in my life? It was good for some, for children who had two decent parents, a good family and cheerful, peaceful minds, who did not have a storm that was constantly blowing day after day.

I have now realised that you can spend your whole life searching for the ideal person to love you. For my part I was failing myself. I was not accepting who I was, and I was building dreams that I knew would never be a reality. What else does a child have? When it has nothing, it only builds on hope. A lot of the time my hope left me and I was empty, because I was not achieving. What I really needed was the healing and the loving of the inner child. You can walk into a shop, and you can read 'Nice to handle, nice to hold, and if broken consider it sold'. Every child is nice to handle and nice to hold, but because I was broken by mother I was like the item that was sold. No one wants a person that is broken; they do not want to take on the responsibility. They want to pass it on to others. When I had my good days, when I tried to be cheerful and happy, Mother was then able to tolerate me, but when I was broken I was someone else's problem. It did not matter who that person was; she just passed me on. I wished people would handle me with delicacy, hold me with tenderness, and if I was broken stay with me and give me love and understanding.

The way my life was lived made me feel at times as if I was an ornament passed from one place to another until I became quieter, more reserved and closed in on myself. You can imagine how I felt as a small child. At this stage I had not even developed my proper personality. I was terrorised and taunted by other children who saw how Mother showed me nothing but scorn. When other people saw her behaving like this towards me it sent out the wrong message, that I was a bold and badly behaved child. In those days parents were always right. Still, at times I was relieved to go to school, it was a change of scenery. When a barrel is empty, it will roll and I was the barrel. I so much desired new outlooks and new hopes but I thought it was all in vain.

When I look back over my life I have a lot of direct anger towards mother. Even when she was not there she was still controlling me because her words were a voice in my mind. They were my control, the complex that she gave me. I could never master skills, because I had an inadequate teacher in Mother who showed me no skills or crafts, only the dark and gloom of life.

As a child when you are traumatised, no matter how down you get, your adrenaline lifts you up, perhaps it is hyperactivity. As an adult you lose it and you can have severe depression for the rest of your life if you do not deal with the inadequacy you suffered as a child. I am sixty-six years old today, I could teach the psychology and physiology of emotions because in my own life, every now and again, wounds are opened by different situations arising. Instead of having one problem I have a hundred to deal with.

My good old Mother's words are knocking at the door , to take over my heart and contaminate it with negativity. God knows that everyone of us at times is tainted with negative thinking. As it says in scripture 'Perfect love drives out all fear'. I got lots of love from Father, but he was hardly ever there as he worked so hard in the fields. Even if I had had the taste of a small amount of love from mother I think it would have been sufficient to get me through some parts of my life. Mother was the one who ruled over me. If she condemned me, I was at fault. If someone praised me I never believed that I was worthy of his or her praise, because mother was the master. She was master of my mind, master of every part of me, and everything I thought or did. Even a reassuring look from her, or a smile upon her face would be sufficient to make me happy all day long at school but if the morning started badly the day was ruined. Even though Mother was never there at school she destroyed my concentration. She ruined me socially and damaged my cognitive development skills.

It is sad that any child should have to experience such deep trauma as this. Mother was the greatest obstacle that ever stood in my path. With her there I could never grow, never achieve, or never succeed. Who could ever live a life like that?

For all of you out there, who have wounds as deep, I pray that you too will be set free; free from the control and domination of a guardian or parent who subdued you, who destroyed your ability to succeed and who gave you qualities that have made you a person today who is insecure and who lives in fear, someone who keeps apologising for no wrong they have done, who cannot live their life to its full potential. The reason I say this is because the past took away my future until God set me free.

The Story of Pet

My aunt Pet was a very gentle and caring lady. She had all the qualities I wanted in a mother and I would often sit in my room and think to myself, 'why hasn't my Mother got those qualities'. It was hard, because not alone did my Mother rule over me, she ruled over the whole household. Nan and Pet were afraid of my mother. Pet went through her own suffering in life as she was an epileptic, and because of it she was victimised. Mother stereotyped her. Pet and I had one thing in common; I had the use of only one eye and Pet had epilepsy.

In my Mother's opinion, if you were not born perfect you didn't deserve to be treated properly. Pet and myself understood each other because we were both treated the same. My heart would bleed for Pet when I used to see the dirty work she had to do but she was able to tolerate the life she was living better than I was. I thought my life was bad but seeing what she had to do made it feel worse. Pet was like a mop machine or a robot; she was always at my Mother's mercy as she was afraid.

Pet used to get endless seizures and my Mother would still have her working in the fields. She never had a tablet inside her mouth as long as she lived. My Mother never even got the doctor for her when she was ill. As with myself, Mother had no compassion for her. Even when she was recovering from her seizures mother never showed her any kindness. I often wondered who would be the next person to come along who would be treated the same way as us. Pet would never budge or give out and did her utmost to keep mother happy.

I have more anger for the way Mother treated Pet, than the way she treated me, because I was Mother's own and Pet wasn't even her relation. I would often wonder whether Mother ever thought about the cruel suffering she caused other people. Did she feel any guilt or remorse for the way she treated Pet and I? If she did, why did she keep doing it? I suppose I think of it in the same light as a thief. A fellow who robs feels guilty for the first couple of times, and then the feeling wears off and he keeps doing it. The guilt dies in him. That's the way my Mother was. She had to have complete control and she was very selfish. She always wanted to slice the cake first and we were like the beggars wanting the scraps, and even that would make us happy.

She made Nan's, Pet's and my lives hell, and she treated us all alike. As I was her own flesh and blood and a minor, wouldn't you think she would have treated me better?

Pet died in the 1970's after a life of severe suffering and a burdensome illness that kept her down. To this day I suffer from guilt at the way Pet was treated, but I know it was not my fault. In Ireland, during that time, anyone with an illness such as epilepsy was treated as if he was in the lowest segment of society and his voice was not heard. Such people were not made to work as hard as Pet, though; Pet had the worst of both worlds by being kept down and made work so hard. My Mother thought that making her work was therapy for her; she wanted Pet occupied so that she did not think about her illness. She was also ashamed of her and would keep her in the field working in case anyone should come into the house.

Now that she is dead I often go to visit her grave because I still feel empty from the way she suffered. When I go to the grave I am filled with peace because I know she is with God and out of her suffering. I hope she has found everlasting happiness with God. I have a shrine in my garden when I pray for people with epilepsy, as I then think of Pet. Pete was very generous; she would give you her heart and she had so little in life.

THE ABUSE THAT HAD NO EXCUSE

I was born to life of freedom
As a wonderful gift to my mom.
One day, her life was taken away,
From here on my life started to decay.
I worked in the fields ,
Which got me my meals.
In barn sheds I did lay
I was tired and I had no say,
I worked as a man ,
When down the hills I ran,
Chasing cattle and sheep,
I was like a shepherd and the flocks I would keep.
My eyes used to weep from the cold and the wind ,
The pains I would feel were like a mighty sting .
I was mocked and laughed at ,
For some of my relations I was a doormat.
I was treated as if I was a piece of steel.
Sometimes like a tractor that had four wheels.
In those fields I would have mighty turns ,
When I came a round I had cold burns
I suffered from fits
And after them my tongue was bitten.
I was afraid to tell
In case they did not believe that I was unwell.
I got no treatment ,
Not even a doctor was sent
Sometimes in my grave ,
I wished I were laid.
I would pray to God to die in the fields.
At least then I would not have to work for my meals.
All I ever received were scraps and peels,
When I lived my life I had no deals.
In my lifetime I got no help,
On my hands I got welts,

They gave me such abuse ,
That nothing could excuse.
I always asked the Lord,
How could I climb the cord.
To get to his land in heaven,
Where I could be happy and live forever.
To my family I was not like a relation,
I did the work of a nation,
I was like the slave or maid of long ago,
And with my family I felt so low.
I could never rise up against evil,
Because inside I would heave.
If you are a person of any race,
You deserve dignity in any case.
If you see someone suffer,
Help them even if you miss your supper.
Help a lonely soul,
And God will give it back to in gold.

My Wonderful Nan

Sometimes it is hard to imagine that people who are not blood relations, like my Nan, can be nicer to you than your own family. You would think your own family would be more supportive but no one except my father supported me. Every child needs a Mother figure in its life as an example and for me that was my Father's stepmother, my Nan. I always ran to her when I was upset.

She always said, 'everything will be ok', and when she put her hand on my head, just the touch of her hand made me warm and gave me a feeling of being loved. If you pet your dog he will be your friend and wag his tail. I was like that little dog, running to Nan for attention. Mother never liked Nan, as they were very different in personality, so she gave Nan the cold shoulder. She never liked me going near Nan, as she was afraid that Nan would teach me a different discipline to hers and she would never accept that. Mother was not alone in controlling me but she controlled my behaviour with other people. I had to choose my words, even as a child, as my mother angered very easily and would use any excuse to discipline me and bring me down.

Nan was like the cornfields because, in going to her, I felt free. It was like a breath of fresh air. Nan died when I was 10 years old and I was so upset that I felt the bottom had fallen out of my life. I cried so much at school that the teacher tried to console me. To this day I have lovely memories of my Nan.

Nan and Pet played a very important role in my life as a child. My life with Nan was really good, even though she suffered. She gave me praise and I enjoyed the fun. Her company was so splendid and she knew that my little heart was tender. She treated me like her child and I knew she loved me.

She had a lovely soft voice and she never said a cross word to me.. I praised God that I had her as a friend and someone to confide in.

God knew that Nan suffered.

She spent long periods in bed I think she suffered from arthritis or 'pains' as they were called in those days. God always joins two broken people together

Nan used to tell me stories about her life and some things would wake you up. She was very trusting with me but I never failed her. We were a protection for one another She did her best to protect me Nan was my stronghold.

THROUGH THE EYES OF A CHILD

When I was 5 years old my mother took me to see an eye specialist because the white scale over my left eye became more noticeable as I got older, and I had no sight in this eye. The doctor said I had a cataract and that I needed an operation to remove it. I went into hospital soon afterwards. Every child at that time thought of hospital as a nice place where they could play with other children but I was scared of it because I was afraid of the operation.

On going into hospital everyone was nice to me and I felt a bit calmer as I sat on my bed. I was shy because I did not know the rest of the children, but I knew when I looked at them from my bed that I would have no problems. I smiled at them and they all smiled back at me. I knew with that smile we could all work together. I settled in and tried to relax as much as I could. Altogether, I spent 6 weeks in this hospital, 6 lonely weeks, which I can still remember to this present day. There was this ward sister whose name was Sr. Rose. I knew by the look on her face that she was not very pleasant and very very unpleasant she was. The other children told me to be wary of her, as she made their lives hard.

A couple of days later I went for my operation. I was put on this little trolley and wheeled up to the operating theatre where they put a mask over my nose. When they put chloroform on it I fought against it because I felt I was going to suffocate and I thought I was going to die. All I could hear was, "hold her down, hold her down." You can imagine how frightening that was for a little child. Then to my horror I discovered the operation was not a success, so I had to go down for another operation and face the same procedure. The doctor was not satisfied, because I had no sight, so I had to go down for the 3rd time. They removed the cataract but the sight was never restored. I was very sore and doped with drugs for pain after the operation. When I was so sleepy and confused I was not really aware of what I was doing, and I wet the bed. When Sr. Rose found this out she was very very angry with me. She laughed at me and mocked me in front of all the children, saying, 'wake up, get your wet sheet off the bed', and then made me parade up and down the ward and tell all the other children that I wet the bed, so they could laugh at me. Then she told me to take my sheet into the next ward, which was the boy's ward and do it again. As I was a shy, quiet little country girl who was very nervous, doing this really embarrassed me. I felt so humiliated that I wanted to run away but I knew I had no way out. My time from then on in the hospital was like hell. I was really terrified of Sr. Rose.

One beautiful sunny day she took me out into the grounds of the hospital and gave me my dinner on a little enamel plate. I looked up at her and I was so nervous of her that I turned the plate over. She had such an evil look in her eyes that it made me shiver. This time she got so cross she made me put the dinner back on the plate including all the dirt and grit. She stood over me and made me eat every bite and I thought at one stage she was going to kill me if I did not eat it. She was a wicked woman.

When Father came to see me I was overjoyed to see him after all I had been through. I begged my Dad to take me away with him and gripped his legs so tightly that I had to be torn away from him. I cried so much I thought I was going to get sick and upset father so much that he did not come to see me again. He could not bear to see me so upset. I longed so much for my Nan to comfort me as well. When I was at home, I used run to her after being abused and put my head upon her lap. She used to put her hand on my head and say lovely soothing words to me. Now I was alone and I had no one to run to when Sr. Rose scolded me. I had a fear of nuns for many years after because of this experience and of hospital

PRAYER

By the power of the hand that created all, be with us O Lord and do not let us fall. Rock our cradles, as we lay awake. Heal us when we have pains and aches. Let Our Lady be our Mother when we have none. Help us to enjoy the fun in our childhood. Help us to crawl, help us to walk, help us to learn your words as we talk. Be our friend and help us always to make amends. Be our Father and comfort us so we do not create any fuss. Give us your wisdom and understanding. Be our God and our King. Let the hand of God that created us give us protection, direction and most of all loving affection.

The Tenderness of A Father's Love

When I was seven years old, I think that I was wiser than any other child was, because I was manipulated so much. I had to advance beyond my years to cope with mental torture and when you learn to behave as I did, it is a hard habit to kick. One of the worst things was the way that Mother twisted my behaviour to tell lies about me, especially to my Father and my Father had always doted on me. I was his favourite child.

When Mother was around, I was nobody's child. I just sat there, hating her lies. Poor Dad, too, had a lot to deal with. All day long, he used to be down on the farm and he had no idea what was going on in the house. I played up to Father, because I wanted his attention, after a hard day with Mother. My Father was less like a Dad and more like a visitor as he worked so hard. I only saw him now and then. I often wished that it were Father who was minding me, as he would say, "You are my little girl Eileen". These words used to give me hope, and I found them uplifting. He used to play games with me and I felt free with Father. I did not worry what he thought of me, as long as Mother was not in the room.

My Father would tell me stories, about animals on the farm and his life as a child. He educated me about many things. Having Father around was like having the peace of God flowing through my heart. I would look up at him sometimes and say, " When are we going on holidays, we can leave the rest of them at home". I said this in front of mother a couple of times, hoping that she would cop on that life was for living, not just existing.

Father would give me 'piggy backs', which I loved. The sense of touch was important to me. It gave me security. At other times, he would catch me by the hand, and swing me around in the field. I used to love to hear him laughing and I think that he enjoyed my company, as much as I enjoyed his.

He sometimes let me take the horses for water and I loved doing this, feeling that I had good control of them. I hated it when he said, "I must go back down to the farm now". I knew then, that it was time for me, to go back to work. Back to Mother for work and discipline.

My Father made a great fuss of me, which I loved. It was wonderful to feel important. Mother knew that I was capable of doing things but she never allowed me freedom, like any other child. God wants every child to be loved and I wished that Mother would love me, the way the animals did.

I would often stand back and, from the outside, I would look in. I would study my Father's behaviour towards the animals and see how he treated them. I also studied the animals, to see their reaction towards Father; Father was fond of all animals, bar horses. I could sit for hours, watching him. It gave me a sense of great peace. I was a child full of enthusiasm; I had to know the why and how of everything that I saw happen. Farming seemed interesting to me as a child, because I did not have much in my life but if I had to farm today, I think I would find it less interesting.

Father made up little stories about the animals and I used to believe that animals had feelings. I was afraid, in case I upset them in any way. I always used a tender voice, when I spoke to them and had a particular love for cows, as I thought they were timid animals. I learned to milk them at a very young age and used to sit on a three-legged stool and sing, while I was milking them. It gave me great joy, as I thought the cows enjoyed my singing and my company. It's funny but when I spoke to the cows and horses they looked at me in a certain way as if they understood. They always gave me the impression that they knew what was ahead of them. I thought that by listening to the stories about the animals I knew what they were going through, and could perhaps find ways to help them. Father was my priority, my number 1, but they were my brothers and sisters, from pigs, to sheep, to cows, to horses. I used to get very angry with my Father when he sent a pig to be slaughtered. I cried after my little friends as I had bonded with them and even given them names. Father used to tell me that slaughtering animals was only putting them to sleep but I knew differently and that he was only trying not to upset me. Father was never blunt. He would always be careful about what he was going to say. However, if Mother told me the same news as Father she would make no effort to think but just come straight out with it. Father always tried not to hurt me in any way. The only time he did was when the animals had to be slaughtered or sold but I suppose farming is farming.

I loved helping father with the sheep, especially in spring when the lambs were being born. You look at a little lamb, as white as snow, so meek and humble, playing games with his brothers and sisters. Living life to the full from the word go. I was like a lamb and Mother was the wolf. God uses the words sheep and lambs so often in the bible because they are such peaceful, calm animals. I was a sheep among wolves but I survived.

My mother had more respect for the animals on the farm than for me. She would give the cats better food. I often wished that I were an animal, because I might get more love. At least they were not beaten as I was. This used to make me jealous because the cats enjoyed every sensation of being loved and I could see it. This craving for Mother's attention was a killer. Looking at the dogs upset me even more because they enjoyed people's attention more than the cats. I would never think of begrudging the dogs love, just because the dogs received it. I begrudged Mother because she never showed it to me.

My childhood was lonely and isolated, my mind was disturbed for want of love, because you grow in love, and with it you develop properly.

Poor Father tried so hard to make a living and to put food on the table. He did his part in contributing to the family, putting in long hours and trying to keep the family together. I think that if he had known the way mother treated me he would have come to my rescue straight away. He would have put a stop to her wicked ways, and life would have been so different for me.

When I sat on Father's lap it was like heaven. He was so gentle, and told me always that 'I was a child worth rearing'. I was confused because Mother kept telling me I was useless. Sometimes I would show up Mother, when father was nice to me. When I was with Father I was like a princess with a crown but as soon as he left, the crown was turned upside down, and the thorns pierced my head.

You can see how different my parents were from each other. Mother was jealous of the attention Father showed me. She wished that all the attention that was ever given to anyone in the world would be given to her. A child needs constant love to feel secure. They are so dependent on adults, and are so defenceless. Mother's constant putting me down, led me to become a broken adult. Because of her, I was very insecure. Thank God I had Father, to relieve me sometimes from the suffering I felt.

All through my life my father was a great role model and I often wished I had his qualities. I looked up to him ,because I desired so much that mother would treat me with love, just as he did. Mother could never showed me any love, it was my sisters who received it all.

One day when I was very upset going to school father gave me a hug and said 'Everything will be ok Eileen' .

I was only 6 years old but I remember it as if it was yesterday. That is why I always went to my father for love.

Father knew in later years that I never received any love from mother, which is why he tried to make it up to me with the love she never gave me.

He tried his best to make up for mother's faults Father tried to lead the way for all of us and at times it got him down.

He was a man who had his own problems, as Mother was very difficult to live with.

She tried to make me like herself, but I rejected this in every way I never wanted to be like her, and definitely not driven by her possessive intentions.

35

MY DADDY HOW PRECIOUS
HE WAS TO ME

My daddy how precious he was to me,
The most beautiful daddy, that ever be,
By a touch of his hand, I knew I was loved,
Not like mother, who always made me disturbed.
From the cradle, I always wanted to be at his side,
For he was the only person in whom I'd confide.
Always on me were mother's eyes
She was my thorn bush who made me cry.
A precious father is a wonderful thing
My daddy made me feel like a king.

MOTHER

When I used to sit at the table, Mother would give me an awful stare, and say 'take your elbows off the table now', but when I was small, I used my elbows to support myself on the table, as the table was too high for me. She would never allow me to start eating until everyone else had started. If I did not eat everything that was on the plate, I was sent out to the farmyard and beaten. To this day I have to finish my plate whether I like the food or not. I am still controlled by her words. I did not like some of her cooking, and sometimes I can still get that horrible taste in my mouth that I got when I ate it. Every child dislikes some kind of food but because of the fear that she drove into me, I had no choice but to eat what was before me even if I felt sick.

I was made set the table at a very young age, and, if I made a mistake, Mother would never correct me there and then. She would wait till the whole family was present, including the workmen. Then she would make a joke of me, and mock me, but Father always stood up for me. I always associate food with bad experiences. The reason I never liked eating at the table was because I was humiliated so often. Normally having a meal with a family is a happy experience. As it says in the musical of Oliver Twist, 'Food glorious food'. Food makes people happy because it fills emptiness. Food never gave me fulfilment, as I was always upset at the table.

All my life, I knew my Mother was a hurt woman and inside she felt deep pain. I knew this because of the expression on her face when she was giving out to me. In later life I think she thought that I could not accept her. Mother had a life-long negative impact on me and I was like a tower crumbling every day, block my block. As I grew up I found it hard to build myself up again. I could not stand being alone, so my theory was: "Leave home, get married and get a quick education". I would have fallen into any man's arms just to feel loved and wanted and I was very lucky that my prayers were answered and that I met Brian.

I always felt that my Mother believed that she was unloved and unwanted by my Father and that this was a burden on her shoulders. One day when I was nine years old I heard her murmuring words to this effect to herself: "He does not love me." On my wedding day when she fought with me, it was as if a knife was piercing her own heart with memories of a marriage that did not live up to her expectations. It also killed her that I met a higher standard of man than she ever thought I would. You can only keep someone down for so long until your own tactics go wrong and that's the way it was with Mother. She was a bully and a manipulator, and when I was a child she manipulated me. Treating me the way she did was like an addiction with her.

At times she tried to turn me against my own Father, but of course she never could. Then she tried to turn my Father against me and my Father sometimes gave in to her because he was afraid of her anger. When she let a roar it could be heard fields away and it made me tremble. My Father said that: "Her shrill voice was like a needle piercing his heart" so you know where my fear started - it started from my Mother.

Some people love being a child but all I wanted was to be free and to grow up. In later life what made me become a nurse was the fact that I had suffered so much as a child and so could understand suffering and give the love to others that I never had. It gave me fulfilment, as I knew I was capable of loving despite never having received it.

Later in life, I kept many parts of my life hidden, especially the sufferings I had endured. It was as if I had a cap on my head, covering my face; so that I could hide under it. Thanks be to God when I was little I had Father when he came up from the farm. God is love and truth, but I saw no truth as a child in suffering. He said that He carried me but what did he mean by this, when my suffering was endless? My life goes on with painful memories that even today unfold. Healing is a gradual process, you must expel painful memories one by one, unlike a computer that downloads everything at once.

Trusting in God was my only hope, whether I thought He existed or not. What else do you put your hope in when you see no light. My only light was my belief. The mind is a very powerful weapon; it can lift you up, or lower you down. Jesus has changed me from a stone that was no purpose to a stone that He now uses to build a house.

Everyone feels anger towards God – even me. We do not understand His ways, because of our limited intelligence. If God were to give man any more than he has, he would try and control what belongs in God's realm.

All my life, I have tried to cross the river, whether it was by rafts, barrels or whatever but I never reached the other side until I was fifty years old. I knew God by now, and I knew He was powerful. I was not His vessel when I floated across the river from side to side but I am now his vessel, and I carry God's people from the water banks, where they have nearly drowned, to the dry banks on the other side.

Every person that turns to God has a role, because God chooses him to do His work. The work is to let other people know the truth about God, and the need for conversion in the world. Just as in a food chain, everyone then would know about God. We can all reach out in the love of God, because it enlightens our hearts.

A BEAUTIFUL MOTHER IN MY LIFE
SHE HAD FAILED

As you can see from my mother I suffered from fear
My mind of torture never was clear.
Down my face those painful tears.
Every little word was ringing in my ears.
Repeating those nasty words I could not take.
It was just like another flake.
The agony was so excruciating and so hard.
I felt I had no adult near me to guard.
My tender body that should have been a shell.
To protect me from harm instead it was hell.
In the fields of corn many times I dazed.
Of a wonderful mother in sight I would gaze.
My life was more than a hazy sunshine.
So many different combinations to combine.
In my heart I had an evil mother's impression.
About everything I had to use my own discretion.
Sooner or later I knew I had to grow up and be smart.
Because as you can see,in my life mother had no special part.
She caused me a lasting pain, which I endured.
And into her manipulation I no longer wanted to be lured.
A mother of love, peace and kindness should have hailed.
But unfortunately in my life she had failed.

An indefinable feeling of
recieving and then being taken

Everybody likes to receive a present at sometime in his or her life especially a child. It uplifts their spirits and gives them an indefinable feeling that makes them special. That is the way I felt when I received a present from Aunt Mamie, who was my godmother. Delight was in Mother's eyes as Aunt Mamie handed me the present and said 'Eileen this is for you, I was all excited, like a dog wagging his tail and with his eyes filled with delight at seeing his owner coming home .I was more excited because I did not get presents very often. Am I worthy of such a thing, I asked myself? I always thought I was a bad girl who did not deserve a present or anything. I took it ,saying, 'thank you very much', and looking to mother for reassurance ,to make sure it was ok; although one thing for sure ,I had no fear getting a present even when mother was there.

In front of mother it was nice to see that someone appreciated me, because I knew mother did not. I also thought it would make her change, seeing someone else give a damn about me .It was not really a present I wanted as a child. I thought more about what mother thought of me than anything else in life. I knew I was not important to her, I was the outcast of the family.

After my aunt left I opened my present with excitement. Mother was standing over me with a smirk on her face. She had no problem seeing me open the present, but the moment she saw that I got red ribbons and a toy she grabbed them. The pull on my hand was like the force of a major tractor. I did not even get the chance to grip it, before it had gone out of sight. Mother played her little act again; she allowed me to receive a present, but I was mot allowed to keep it.

As I was so small and mother so tall, it took some energy to look up to her. Your mother is someone you look up to even when you stop growing. For myself, I could never look up to her because of the look in her eyes. Even when I did grow up,

I could not live up to her standards, boundaries or limits. After this event she got the idea into her head that I was evil. I think mother was full of guilt, and the guilt was making her what she was. Mother was like a thief who feels terrible about the house he robbed the night before, and shows great concern when people hear and talk about it. H e asks who might have robbed the house, hoping people will not think it was him and tries to cover his own tracks. Mother was like this she knew she was the apple that was bad and sour and inflicted that punishment on me because of her own shame.

It made her feel good to bring me down. Mother was capable of loving giving and caring and had all the good qualities of a mother because she showed it to the rest of the family. She just chose to treat me differently. Maybe she did not bond with me when I was born. There was no excuse for the way she treated me. Jesus said 'Love one another as I have loved you'.

The only person that ever showed me love was my dad. On the day I received my present of the ribbons and my toy ,mother even tried to turn dad against me. I ran to my Daddy when she took my present off me..

I wanted him to receive me with open arms, as I was so upset, and the smile on father's face made me so happy. I told him the whole story about what mother had done and my father tried his best to console me.

Then all hell broke loose, because I had told him and he went to confront mother. He could not understand why a mother would take a present from a child just like that.

Mother hated me before, but now she despised me for sharing her little secret She could not accept the fact that someone else knew how evil she was,

She was very embarrassed in front of father and I could see the remorse in her eyes for what she had done. That day she was so angry that my whole heart was on fire from all the threats and abuse.

Then father went away again and I was left in her company. Father was a quiet man, and when he had said his piece he would go away again. He was a man who wanted to live in peace; He would not fight with anyone.

Mother growled at me all that day like a dog.

She said so much to me how evil I was, and that she was going to tell all my aunts about me, Then I started to believe it myself. The impact of this was to leave me with no sense of self worth and to believe that I was nobody. I was the lost child searching for the perfect mother. I had to realise no such luck existed.

From that day on, I could never receive presents from anyone in the way I should. I do not feel the same, because, for me, the meaning and the feelings for a true gift are gone. People give out of love, but although I know they are full of good intentions, the feeling still hangs over in my mind and the memory of it opens up floodgates when I get presents.

I believe that mother suffered in her own life and because of her suffering she blamed me. When we suffer in life, we have to release it somewhere, on something or some other person. This was mother's way of coping. After the effect it had on my life, despite my innocence, I hope that I would never cause anyone else to suffer. God says, 'In the world do not become materialistic', because the greatest energy you can spend on presents is better spent in letting people know about God. Then they will receive joy, love, peace and hope. God is better than all the gold in the world. What he gives, He gives freely. I see Jesus and God as my present ; as scripture says, 'I found a treasure in a field that no one else can steal', and it's true, not even my mother.

My eyes sparkled with delight

When I saw my Aunt Mamie in sight,
A beautiful present for me, I was so pleased,
My heart, so troubled by Mother, was at ease.
A little glimpse of hope, even if it only lasted for a moment,
A beautiful present for me was meant.
I felt important that I was thought of once,
 Even if I received nothing for another 12 months.
Handed a present, I took it with a smile,
I looked at my aunt and thanked her very much for a while,
I wanted mother to see that I was grateful.
Just for a second I was hopeful.
Mother might see that I was precious in other people's eyes,
And would not inflict pain on me over presents and toys.
For a minute I thought I was a king,
Glad of anything anyone would bring,
Just to boost my self worth it was great,
I thought it would be a turnaround.
Maybe I could have faith,
Faith in mother that I would be no longer be a maid,
And not be an anchor for her suffering or her aid,
That for one day I could be a princess,
And not look at a woman that was stressed,
And always putting me to the test.
From my hands she grabbed my present with force,
My little red ribbons that I had received, now had no source,
I knew I would not be getting them at a later course.
I was like a child that had no voice,
Everything I said was only hoarse.
The tears I cried were never dried

Because my Mother would not take my side.
My loving Father, into his arms I ran upset,
What mother had done I told him it was like a death.
Consoled by daddy, who was my only comfort,
I felt at times I could fly to him like a bird,
He was so peaceful, calm and collected,
Different to mother, by her I was infected,
Saying to me I was evil because of her own guilt.
I was innocent, but inside me fear she had built.
I had no courage, no self-esteem and no confidence,
From different vibes I thought at times I was dense,
My lasting present now, is my Lord, my Saviour,
At least God does not treat me with such bad behaviour.
He has given Himself to me as a lasting treasure, which I did find,
And no one can steal it, even mother, He is so kind.

WATCHING VISITORS

I loved climbing trees, because I would be the first to see any visitors coming into the farmyard. I was a very curious child, and I always wanted to know what was going on and to be involved in what was happening, especially when visitors called. Mother always excluded me and when I climbed the trees, it gave me a great buzz, because I could see the people coming in, before Mother did. Usually, if I were in the house when people called, she would tell me to get out. As soon as the visitors went inside I would come down from the tree, sneak around the house to see if there was an open window and to listen to Mother, to see if she was putting me down again.

I was paranoid about Mother, which is why I would creep and crawl around the house, inside and out, eager to hear what she said about me. She did not know what I knew and I could have no love for this woman who did what she did. Because I knew, I would at times act in a certain way and she could not understand my behaviour. She used to say, " My other three children are so easy to rear, they are no trouble, but Eileen I cannot train. My heart is broken from her, beating her with a stick does not seem to work. She is nothing but a troublemaker. She has my heart broken. That was Mother, my own flesh and blood. All my life, I wondered, why I was her enemy? Why, her forbidden fruit? The reason for her hatred towards me, I will never know.

FORBIDDEN FRUIT

The life I lived was dangling from a tree,
Whatever way the wind was blowing, it affected me,
I took it as it came, as it was all the same,
I tried to change Mother, but she tried to change me.
Many falls did I have, from that old oak tree.
I hoped God would be my navigator,
Because, after all, He was my creator.
I climbed the tree, to take my legs off the ground,
So up in the tree, I would feel safe and sound,
I was like the bird, coming and going, in search of something else,
Chocolate was not the thing that was put into my mouth to melt,
Only words were used, to make my jaw tense,
I was always trying to protect myself in my defence.
I lived in fear, so most of the time I was hanging,
I knocked on the door of heaven, I kept banging,
I never gave up, or ran away,
Because with my hope, in God I remained brave,
I found the Lord in the right place in my life,
And with His power He helped me strive.

In The Cornfields

When I was about 7 years old my Father made a swing for me. He tied a rope between 2 trees and I was so happy and so grateful to him. One day I was sitting on my swing, swinging backwards and forwards, when my sister appeared around the corner of the house and said, 'Mother wants you for work'. I stayed on swinging for a few more minutes when, all of a sudden, my mother appeared; she was so angry that I ran away from her, and in fear and terror I jumped over the ditch and into a cornfield. I was fearful and afraid of the dark. The field was empty and I felt alone in the world. As I walked in through the entrance, briars cut me. My wounds were deep and some of the thorns were left in my legs. It was very stupid to jump because my conscience told me not to and I didn't listen, and the result was I was all cuts and bruises. As children everyone knows we all like to lick our wounds and be in our mother's arms.

My Mother thought I should not cry and should be hard, and hard she made me, but I knew inside this wasn't me. I just wanted her to greet me with open arms and tell me everything was ok, when I was upset. All I wanted was re-assurance. As I walked through the field of gold, I felt it was heaven, the corn was the colour of the sun. I wanted to run and break free through the cornfield; I wanted to act upon this freedom of choice. There would be nobody to boss or shout at me, and, please God, the owner would never see me because I felt I could hide. That wonderful feeling was my own little world. I could hear sounds but nothing could be seen. I suppose it was the bees collecting honey, and the birds, were singing and that was how I felt. I wanted to be happy and to be like the birds and not be seen.

When you think of the cornfields you think of the sunshine. It`s as if God in heaven has done His work. The colour of the corn is in His image. It was my light and that's why I called to the cornfields. The bright sun is what makes people happy. I always loved brightness. If I had my way my roof would be of glass so that the sun could shine through. I suppose when I look back now it was like dancing in heaven. It was freedom. With the Lord I felt free.

When I looked all around I could see acres of corn in every direction. It was endless and in a way it was a touch of heaven. My mind was infected with so much darkness that when I saw the colour of the cornfields it was like a lamp shining through me. Once again I had light and that light made my face smile. When I looked up at the clear blue sky it reminded me of the sea, it was so peaceful, so soothing and so calm. I felt that this was the only heaven I would ever see. These happy memories have stayed with me my whole life. When we are in our darkest moments struggling through life, we look back to our childhood and think about what made us happy back then. Thinking about the cornfields gives me a lift because I remember what made me cope. Being in the cornfield was a new life for me, being born.

Then came the call that made me shiver; it made my head spin and my legs turn to jelly. I could feel it in my heart; it was so sharp you might as well have stuck a dagger in me. Its amazing how simple words can affect you by the tone used for them. You need never guess who made them. It could only be my mother. The threats of blackmail against my father made me so upset that I just wanted to say, ' Mother, if you catch me any more I will run from you and I will fight even more for freedom'. The threats were so powerful, I was like a bee buzzing. I asked myself what was it all for. My lovely sisters were like angels who could do nothing wrong. I took the punishment for them. Mother took all her frustration out on me. I gently walked toward her and did as I was told. I felt my mind was absent from my body. I was so driven by fear that it brought me to a different land, a land of the unknown. As I walked towards her, every step I took was like a heart attack; this woman terrified me.

I longed so much for the love of a mother and I used to try and make myself believe that my mother was different. I tried to picture her as a loving, caring mother and no matter what she did I kept this image. This image is called survival.

As I looked into her face I could see the look of bitterness and spitefulness; she was unforgiving and uncaring. She was growling at me and I wanted to look away; being on another planet was my only way. The little smirk on her face every now and then was the cruellest, it was her way of showing who was boss. I looked down at her feet; I couldn't take the confrontation, and I did not know why my life was as hard as it was. I was like a king of cherry blossom, growing if my mother gave me any compliment, because they were very few in my childhood. When she treated me badly, it was like walking on a bed of thorns, and, to cope, I used to build images of goodness to help me defend myself in my battle. You would never imagine that fear could make you sick. Fear affected me in my childhood and has affected me to this very day. Fear is funny. If you suffer from it your immune system goes down and you can pick up any kind of sickness or illness. My fear was not just the event of a moment. It was ongoing. Fear made me shiver and I was afraid of my own shadow. When I looked into the mirror I used to ask myself some questions. Why be born if only to be controlled by someone else? Many times I ran into the cornfields. I was fascinated by the idea of hiding. On this terrible occasion I got very sick as a result of the fear; my appetite went down, I used to get cold sweats and I was nearly incontinent.

My head was always down; I was more like a maid in the house than a daughter and I never understood how she could treat me so badly. In a way I was glad I became sick because it made my mother afraid, and through her fear, in case anything serious happened to me, she showed me kindness. How I wished it was a lasting one. It was for her own ego that she showed me kindness at this time. The minute I was better the leopard regained his spots. The colour of the corn gave me hope because I knew life existed through the beauty of nature. I knew that there was something out there that was more powerful than my mother, and that she could not take it from me. It is funny that if you are affected the way I have been at the hands of my mother you look for beauty in other things and live on a day to day basis. You do not look years ahead of you because you know that surviving one more day of hardship is a miracle.

This particular day is still in my memory as if it was yesterday and it makes me realise that fear of my Mother has always controlled me. It is like a disease that she has passed on to me. It has taken me most of my life to realise that this was a chain that tied me down, but the links have been broken one by one and I am getting there. It interfered with my marriage, particularly in the early years, but now that I have come into the light I can understand it. Jesus said, ' in me there is no darkness', and, now that I am united to Jesus in prayer, these bonds do not hold me back.

I forgive my mother but at a very expensive cost. I do not understand why she treated me like the maid, instead of one of the family. I am not perfect or near perfect but no matter who you are, everyone deserves love. Love is what makes us whole. It gives us the strength and the ability to go through life, to be positive and trusting and to live in hope.

People, never let your life be controlled by fear. Face the fear and God's mighty power will come to your aid. If you want to break free and come into His light, God lifts you up and places you in His loving arms. Fear comes from man controlling man; God never taught us to fear. There is an awesome fear when you first get to know God. This is called the good fear. Anyone who starts something new is afraid but when you get to know God everything is giving and hope. Praise His Holy name!

God's little angels

All through my life I had little angels at my side,
Through frustration and irritation they were my guide.
Through the tears and sadness I cried,
God's little angels came to me like the tide,
Crying and pleading, to them I would reach for my peace
Without this inward peace my life would cease.
Stay on her side was the right thing to do,
Otherwise with her anger into the room you'd go,
Freedom I cried freedom I shouted,
In my life no more did I need to doubt,
Looking back I was held up, when mother held me down,
With wonderful angels from heaven who had crowns,
Little angels as white as snow
Gave me everything to help me flow,
My sweet little angels you are my angels so sweet.

If I Were Born Again

If I were born again, it would be without sin,
A life without burdens from beginning to end,
Away from Mother and sisters,
At times I felt that I would not miss her
And all the cruelty and the agonising pain.
I was like a dog; I needed to be tamed
And for everything that happened in my life I was blamed,
For everyone else it was not the same.
I hoped the mirror of Mother, would never reflect me,
They say like our parents, we must be,
But If I were like Mother, I would not have coped,
I prayed to God I would be different; that is what I hoped.
With father at least, my life had a different scope,
And it is Jesus now, who I look up to as my Saviour,
I knew with God, that He has no favourites.

BEHIND THE TRUTH LIES A TERRIBLE PAST

Behind the truth lies a terrible past. It is funny how our lives reflect the life of Jesus and hard to believe how we follow Jesus, through different ways. Jesus said, 'If you want to be a disciple of mine follow me', and it is amazing how our lives follow Him, before we reach the truth. It is what we do with the truth that changes our lives. I was once a captive but now I am free. Free to preach the word of God and free to do His works. If I did not have a past I would not have the love I now have for God. So really, when you think about it, even having a past seems a failure it's not a failure if you can turn it around and that goes for everyone. My past, you could say, was a failure because of the way I suffered; it was not the glory of God at work but it was the hand of God that turned my life around. We are born to praise the glory of God. God has a covenant with us before we are born. We are His children and in Him only shall we trust. It is wonderful to have received the message of God because it helped me.

When I think of countries where God is not known, it makes me sad. They have horrendous lives without any hope. It is the hope that keeps us sane, and gives us the will to live. It lifts the burdens off our shoulders and sets us free. People do not realise the value of hope. Even if what we dream about does not come true, at least we can still look forward to a future of peace, prosperity and freedom in hope. The rose of hope, just like the flower itself when it is in season, yields to God and flowers with glory. Its testing time is during the hardship of winter and the frost and that is the way my life has been. I was a briar and now I am a rose in colour and in season. Praise the Lord, Alleluia! The Lord has fed me with His word, month by month, year by year. His word is my food and nourishment. Just as with the flower blossoming, I sometimes feel like a flower as it does in the winter and I ask myself, 'where is God` but he is always at my side, not far away. God is a God of love, he gives us love and in love we grow

The Innocent Rose

One morning a little rose bud opened to yield to the sun,
It opened its petals, so beautiful in colour, one by one,
Absorbing all the nourishment from earth it could take.
That's was the reason from its sleep it became awake,
It smelt like perfume that was so sweet,
 And every moment of its life was God's beat.
In the cold it shrivelled up and went back to sleep,
And in those days it stayed humble and meek,
Waiting for the sun. It was very patient,
Trusting in the Lord it had no hesitation,
Never complaining, doing what it was told
 Because the little flower knew it was God's mould.
If we were all little flowers we would have seasoning,
And to our lovely God we would be very pleasing.
We would not mind being cold or even freezing,
Because, during our trials, God would give us easing.
When you think of a flower think of yourself and others,
Tell them of the flowers so that they too can be your brothers.

The animals on our farm my mother paid more respect to.
She would give the cat better food than me. I often wished that I
was an animal because I might get more love, al least they were
not beaten I was. This used make me jealous. The cats enjoyed
every sensation of been loved and I could see it. The craving
for my mother 's attention was a killer. I so longed to be loved
even looking at the dog's upset me more because they appreciated people's attention more than cats. I would never think of
begrudging the dogs love just because the dogs received it, but I
begrudged my mother because she never showed it to me.
    My childhood was lonely and isolated, my mind was dis-
turbed in the want of love because you grow in love and without
it you do not love.

I am a great lover of animal. I loved all the animals on the farm when I was small. I had a great love for cows as I always thought they were very timid animals. I learned to milk them at a very young age. I used to sing while I was milking and it gave me great joy as I thought the cows enjoyed my singing and my company. The only animals that I was afraid of were horses. I still have a fear of them today. My father was a little bit harsh on them and I think that is what made me afraid. The animals were great company to me as a child as I was always on my own. The ducks and hens were like a family to me .I loved feeding them. Then I would collect the eggs from the different fowl gouses

Another time I went and told the animals my problems, and I think that they listened. Whatever about animals I felt comforted in my sorrow. It was like the whole weight of the world lifted from me. but the day after would be just as bad.

I often thought if I fell off a wall, it might be an easy solution to my problems. I cannot understand how god left me live in this miserable world. To look around in the world, used make me distressed. To look within, always made me depressed. To look up caused me to be blessed.

My life was no blessing, nothing but a messing. Whether I looked up, or down in or out it was the same everyday. No matter how many times I asked God for help when I was heavily burdened, I felt that He never answered me. Why give me a life, when he could not maintain it?

All the years that went past, I still felt the same. All the pain and all the grief nearly drove me insane. My mother told me that I must not grief over anything. I tried to look forward, beyond earth's shadows. I could never idly stand. It was like that there was no rest for me on this land. Mother was the bow, and from it everyone else fired his or her arrows from it. Whatever mother thought of me, It was how other people judged me. If she was nice, people were nice to me. When she was horrible, everyone else was horrible.

Feeding the Animals

I loved working with Father, but one job I hated was going out with him at night to feed the horses. I never complained, because I loved his company. My job was to hold the lantern, so that he could see where he was going, because we had no electricity in the 1940s. He used to feed them with barley and oats, which he kept in an outhouse, but because of the feed, this house was full of rats. When I went in with my lantern, I could see them scurrying around, their little claw feet making a tearing sound. I was terrified, and I wondered how the cats got away with not doing their job which was clearly to rid us of farmyard rats. Father, sensing my reluctance to go into the sheds would call the dogs to chase the rats, but he never quite knew just how terrified I was. I was not in the habit of admitting I was afraid.

In the springtime, I loved the new life, especially during lambing time. If a sheep had more than two lambs, and did not have sufficient milk to feed them, we brought that little lamb into the kitchen, and fed it with a bottle and teat. The bottle was usually an empty coffeee bottle, (Irel coffee) and a special large teat. One of the lambs became a pet and followed me everywhere. I became like Little Bo Peep and her little lamb. I christened my new companion Nancy. One day I was putting out the clothes, and while I was bending over, up came Nancy and hoisted me into the air. When Nancy had to go to market I hugged her to death. I cried for weeks after her.

We always kept pigs and, when the sow was ready to have her piglets, I used to hope she would have them during the day, in case I was told to hold the lantern by night. I always knew when the mother sow was about to have her piglets, as she would start to make her bed. She was put in a house by herself, with a bed of straw and used to chop up the straw with her mouth, and tease it out with her feet. When she had her bed made to her satisfaction she would start to give birth. The litter of small pink piglets could be anything from ten to twenty. The sow could never be left on her own, when she was producing her piglets, because if she felt like it, she would give a loud grunt, stand up, and flop down again. We had to be on constant guard, to watch out for the piglets, in case she suffocated them when she flopped. We cleaned each little piglet as soon as it was born with straw, and then put it on to the mother's breast to help it find its own teat. I never liked the squeak of the piglets and the mother sow used to grunt so often that I wondered quite frankly if she was ever cut out for motherhood. I was always afraid in case she ate her little brood, an passtime some sows indulged in.

I loved fowl and in order to hatch her chickens a hen had to get the hatching urge which was called "clucking". She would make a peculiar noise, and her feathers would feel very full. The clucking motivated her to sit on a nest of eggs for up to three weeks without getting off, except to get water or feed. This was an amazing feat of endurance. Mother would put a dozen eggs into a box, then put in her clucker, and remove the lid from the box every day at feeding time. At the end of three weeks, the little chickens would break through their shells. They were lovely, - soft, fluffy and yellow. The hen looked after her chickens with great care, and she would cover them all with her wings. If you tried to play with her chicks, she could give you a nice peck, and look up at you, as much as if to say: "Mind your own business." Sometimes when we had a surplus of cluckers, Mother would put them to hatching duck eggs. I used to peep into the box every day waiting to see my lovely, fluffy, yellow ducklings. I was always amazed that as soon as they were born they seemed to love water. The turkeys and geese also produced little yellow goslings, and little grey turkey chicks. I never took to the turkey chicks, but I loved the yellow goslings. I was afraid of the gander because if you got too close to the goose and her goslings he could chase you with great vehemence around the yard. He would stretch out his long neck, flap his wings and make a loud noise. If you did not get away quickly he would peck you and it would be no soft peck either.

I loved to watch the ducks, and little ducklings wash and swim in the stream that ran through the farmyard. I have a special love for ducks, and I love to hear them make their "quack-quack" sound. The hens had their own house, and the geese, ducks and turkeys had their own separate homes to live in. The ducks would come home very late at night as they wandered throughout the farm, and enjoyed the little streams and wells. I was always terrified in case the fox would kill them. We always made the fowl houses secure at night, in case the fox broke in and caused havoc among the chicks. The little chicks had many predators and had to be protected from hawks as well.

Our hens were muli coloured, so we had great variation in our fowl. They consisted of many breeds; dark red ones called Rhode Island Reds, black hens called Back Minorca, White Leghorns, which were white and skinny and White Sussex, which were fluffier, and seemed to have bigger wings. We also had Bantams, which were very small, just a little bit bigger than a pheasant, and Guinea hens, which were like small turkeys and cackled all day. The noise they made was like ' hearing "two O' clock, two o' clock" over and over. When the hens had laid eggs in their nests, they came out of their houses with a loud cackling noise and the cockerels, too, always made sure they were heard. So, as you can see, the farmyard in those days, between the animals and the fowl, was full of life.

Birds were another form of life that enthralled me. They used to build nests in our trees, which were situated at the back of the house. In wintertime, when we had snow, there were a great variety of birds and I was fascinated by the colour of the plumage. I used to feed them with scraps of bread and watch them perch on the branches of the trees as they proudly surveyed everything with their sharp eyes. I always envied them their freedom. If they were in trouble they could fly away. The idea of flying out of danger used to give me a lovely safe feeling inside.

I used to wish God would give human beings wings to make us like angels. I loved watching the birds gliding through the sky and just looking at them put my heart into an ecstasy and gave me a great sense of peace and tranquility. When birds sit on a branch they watch to make sure there is no danger lurking, so that their little chickens will be safe. They protect them from any possible harm. It is wonderful to see how nature protects the vulnerable. It is definitely the hand of God at work. Those little chicks never go hungry and their mother always keeps them warm. I used to say to myself: "If the birds are looked after well, surely to God I am worth more than a bird and I deserve more protection." If they could receive peace in their lives surely I must be worthy of it. Seeing the young birds ready for flight filled me with hope. When they fell they would get up again until eventually their practice and courage resulted in free-flying, air-hovering perfection.

To me, birds were like the messengers of God. They used God's energy to fly. The Holy Spirit descended in the form of a bird and birds have their way of praising God when they sing. I am still half puzzled by a question I often pose to myself: "If I was a bird would I have had a better life?" They have the freedom to fly away and they give us the true message of God's love for us, that we should fly together when things go wrong. God gives us many images in nature to show us how to live our lives to the full. We cannot say that we are not taught.

One of my favourite chores involving nature was taking tea to the men who were working in the fields. No tea ever tasted as nice as the tea in the fields. I still have the taste of it in my mouth.

When the men were finished eating and drinking, I got whatever was left over. I took the tea in a sweet gallon, or else in whiskey bottles. The bottles were put into large men's stockings to keep in warm. Tea, sugar and milk were all mixed together. The sandwiches were made up of home-made brown bread and jam. After the thrashing, my father kept one bag of wheat – this was sent to the mill to be ground into flour. No bread tasted as sweet as this bread.

If mother was in a good mood, she bakes some apple cake and I also took apple cake to the field. The men made themselves comfortable on heaps of hay, if it was the hay season, or sheaves of corn, if it was the harvest time. Then they would tell stories and I would love to listen. When my dad finished his tea, I would ask him for his cup and help myself to tea.

I would then trot home on the mud paths through the fields. I used to watch the little rabbits running about. Sometimes I would see the odd badger but I was a bit fearful of badgers as Dad complained about them damaging the crops. I would look out for pheasants. I loved the colours of the pheasant's foliage. On my way through this paradise I would finally look up at the sky and hear the birds singing loudly as if they were singing a melody especially to me. When finally I glanced again at the grass I could see all the wild flowers spread like an exotic carpet pattern before me with yellow buttercups, white daisies, blue bells and clover.

SUICIDAL THOUGHTS

When I was a child, I remember Father and other farmers used to get sand from the local beaches. They put it on their land as a fertiliser, to grow crops such as wheat, barley and oats. They also used it to grow vegetables, such as turnips, mangles and potatoes.

One day, when Father hired a lorry to get some sand he asked me if I would like to go for a spin, so off I went. When I got there I sat by the seaside while they were filling up the lorry with sand. I sat with my head in my hands weeping, desperate for my life to change. I could hear the ocean as it gushed against the rocks and gaze at the exquisite scenery. Oh! How beautiful it was! What peace, tranquillity and relaxation I felt. I was being elevated to a different world, lifted above my pain, but yet, while water can be so peaceful, it can also be so deadly, because it can take life.

I wanted to jump into the sea, and never come back, because of the pain and inflammation in my heart. It was sore to touch a wound so open, that never had a chance to heal. With ongoing torments and crucifixions how could you expect it to be any different? My tears ran down my face, one by one. I could taste every tear, as it seeped into my mouth and it was saltier than the sand. I shivered from fear and shock at the bitter taste in my mouth. Breathing deeply I had the feeling that I was going to have a heart attack.

I was undecided as to whether I would end my life.

I wanted to enjoy life, and live like every other kid. The life I was putting up with was not living. My pain was Mother's gain, and why was I sitting here suffering for it? When I saw other children laughing and playing on the beach my tears came faster. I was getting such sniffles, that I could barely breathe. The cold sea air was blowing against my face and I felt as if it was winter. Out of boredom I picked up pebbles, and threw them one by one, to ease my frustration. Then, taking off my shoes, I glided my feet along in the sand. There was a great feeling of relaxation but it did not solve what was going on in my head. I was on the outside looking in; all I could see was darkness, and a hollow. There was no future; all was bleak and I sought to end my life. Night after night I asked God to take me in my sleep. At least then I would have no pain.

The hours passed, and I could now see that the lorry was full of sand. Father called me, in his gentle, kind voice. I ran towards him, and he helped me to get into the lorry. As I looked out of the window, I could see the clouds getting darker, as it came to the closing of the day. The sun went in, and the stars were coming out. I knew that I had survived yet another day and that I was going home again, to face the music, which was a horror story, a life of hell.

The lorry pulled into the farmyard and I rushed indoors as fast as I could. When I entered by the backdoor, there was Mother, sitting by the cosy fire. Her roaring words were, 'why were you so long? You have a lot of work to do'. In an instant, she said, ' clean the kitchen, and wash up the pans,' and I said to myself 'Lovely Mother'. If I had done what I had planned, I would now be out of this hellhole. Although I was tired, I still had to carry on working. I had no choice. Heavily burdened, my life continued on.

The incident at the sea was not the first time I contemplated ending my life. For a child to take his own life, or even to think of it, shows a terrible fear. I had problems, and lots of them. It was as if the weight of the world was on my shoulders. I did not know how I would cope, or how I would get by. People did not realise that my little heart was deeply wounded. They did not understand how I felt, they thought that I was a happy little girl. Often I went out among the animals, and told them my problems. I think they did listen to me. Whatever there is about animals, I felt comforted in my sorrow. It was as if a burden had been lifted from me. But the day after it would be just as bad.

I often thought that if I fell off a wall, it might be an easy solution to my difficulties. I could not understand how God let me live in this miserable world. When I used to look around the farmyard, and see all the work I had to do, I was distressed. Looking within my heart used to make me feel depressed. Looking up at the sky I thought I would be blessed by the power of God.

My life was no blessing. It was all messed up. Whether I looked up or down, in or out, it was the same, every day. So many times I asked God to help me, and He never answered me. He knew I was heavily burdened and I said to myself, 'why, why, did God give me a life, if He could not maintain it'? The pain and the grief nearly drove me insane.

My mother taught me not to cry over anything. I tried to look forward beyond earth's shadows. I could never stand idle because there was no rest for me in this land. Mother was the bow and from it every one else fired their arrows. Whatever opinion she created about me others had to follow.

A CHILD WHO SUFFERED

I was crucified which made me think of suicide,
A thought that never left my side,
It put me in despair
My little mind was gone, beyond repair.
I had learned a path of negative thinking
And it caused my ship to start sinking.
I could find no reason why I wanted to live,
Or how much more to this life I should give
Another day was dawning
Because of yesterdays work I was yawning.
Every minute lasted days ,
When I could I was in a daze
Of this that and the other
How could I change mother?
I tried changing myself, deep within,
Because I believed I was living in sin.
I treated her with tenderness, with quietly spoken words,
But all I would get back, was a dagger or a sword.
Streams of painful tears, would rush from my eyes
A wicked word can destroy someone's; character,
And each day, part of me was eaten more and more.
My good old name had, had its death
Facts are facts, mother had her pets.

PLEADING FOR MERCY

Pleading for mercy, to our Sacred Jesus Christ is so important. It sets our loved ones free, not alone for those who are living, but also for the deceased. Pleading for mercy for anyone, in any kind of trouble, because of sin, can transform that person. Even if they are not praying, they can feel touched by the power of God in different ways.

The power of prayer for one another must be united with love for our sisters and brothers. God is the merciful one, but we too can show the mercy of God, by forgiving, by letting go of grudges, and by being pleasant. In today's world, mercy is never spoken about. Without mercy, we cannot go to the next level with God. God shows us mercy, even when we have turned from the wrong road, and through His mercy we are put on the straight path.

God is living among us, but if God were here in person, He would forgive us and show us mercy. When you have seen those principles carried out, by your own eyes you will learn how important it is, to do unto others, what God has done, unto you. The season of Advent, is the season of good will. If for years, or months, you have been holding grudges, turn to your friends today and say I forgive you.

Forgiveness is an act of the heart, which must be followed by an act of the mind. After forgiveness, comes mercy. In society today, the mind is always in opposition to the heart. People lose control and that is where discernment comes in. Discernment is a gift for anyone in their own lives, to help them make decisions, and follow the right path.

Just remember if Jesus has taken control of your heart he can also inspire your mind, but your mind can still be led in two ways, for God or against God. God's Spirit is a very powerful force; it is a spirit moving within us and around us. It lights a fire in the darkest parts of our hearts and it is our battery when we are flat.

When we are baptised in the Spirit, the waters of heaven open, and we are washed clean. We become part of God. Years ago, back in Jesus' time, we all know that Jesus himself was no sinner. He knelt on the ground, and pleaded from His heart to God the Father, and joined His hands in prayer. That is what we should do. People need to start adoring God more, pleading with God, the all-powerful, awesome channel at His source. No matter how great the sin or sinner, this is the direct root to change.

Remember Jesus is the Ocean of Divine Mercy; He heals your wounds, and makes every part of you clean. He makes you feel unique. His hands will uphold you and you will never stumble, because He will walk with you. ' Let not your heart be troubled, or your mind upset' (John 14) A troubled mind must surrender to its loving God and in its place, God will put hope, light and faith. You will be led from the life of hell, to His life of joy.

Plead for mercy for there is no such greater power. You can make a life that was sour in the past, better. The greater the sinner, the greater the mercy. Come away today from your life of debauchery.

WANDERING LABOURERS

When I was a child growing up in the 1940s, wandering labourers, tramps, and what were known as 'characters', roamed the countryside. One of these was ' Mad Lynch'. He was mentally ill, and just walked through the fields, from house to house, begging for food. I was absolutely terrified of him. I used to see him eating his overcoat and one large corner of it was eaten away. I do not know to this day whether it was hunger or madness, or both, that made him behave like that.

Mother was very kind to this man, and always offered him food. She told me she knew his background and that he had emigrated to America as a young man, only to find, when he came home years later, that all his family had died from TB. The family farm had been sold and he was so upset that he started to walk through the countryside, until it became his lifestyle. When Mother gave him food, he used to eat with his fingers and very fast. Just looking at him frightened me. His speech was incoherent and he had a dreadful look of evil in his eyes.

Another character, who called at intervals, was Calnan. He was a very gentle, kind old man, always spoke with a soft voice and loved children. He used to tell me stories while I sat on his knee and I was never afraid of this man. He wore a big black hat where he carried holy books and always spoke kindly of everyone. His pockets would be full of rosary beads, prayer books and medals and I knew he was a man of prayer, because he was always full of peace. Mother would sometimes make a bed for Calnan in an outhouse but was afraid to let him sleep in the house, as he used to smoke cigarettes. Mother told me that when Calnan was young he studied for the priesthood, but found the studying very difficult and, as a result, had a nervous breakdown. I was amused at some of the things he used to do, such as asking me for a glass of water, breaking medals in two, and swallowing them. Then he would tear some paper out of a holy book, roll it up into a ball, and chew it. I used to wonder about his digestive system! He lived until he was very old and died in a hospital used for the old poor people. Years ago, after the famine, some of those hospitals were called workhouses. Then they were called poor houses and later on community hospitals.

Tom Cullinane was a wandering labourer who would work for a few weeks with one farmer, then move on to find more work, in another area. Tom was a regular visitor to our farm coming perhaps three to four times a year. He had a big problem with lice and Mother used to give him clothes when he arrived and used louse powder on all his bedclothes. Mother always felt, when he was rid of the lice, he would move on. Tom was a very good worker and he and father got on well together.

I came to know a lot of those men, some of whom were very kind, and my father would take on anyone, when he needed extra help on the farm. However, one day a stranger called to the door and asked Father if he needed help. Father took him on immediately and never asked him where he came from. He just asked him if he wanted something to eat, and then set him straight to work. Although I was only eight years old I was a great judge of character and could see something very peculiar in this man. I never made free with him, and did everything I could to stay out of his way. The following Saturday, mother and father went to town as usual to sell chickens, eggs, potatoes, and vegetables at the market. They travelled in a horse and cart. Although they usually used a horse and trap, if they had a lot of potatoes the cart was needed - or long car, as it was called in the country. Dad would fill a bag with soft hay, and that was mother's seat while travelling. This stranger was left in charge of my sisters and I, and my parents were no sooner out of sight than this stranger approached me. I was gripped by fear. I ran into the house, as fast as I could go, and up the stairs. He followed me, saying that he wanted to sing a song for me, as he fancied me, and then said he loved me. I was lucky that my sisters followed me, because they were older than I was and I screamed loudly and cried my heart out. I think he was frightened by my screams. My sisters tried to comfort me and the man eventually left the room, and walked down the stairs. I still remember it clearly. Perhaps he had no intention of abusing me, but with my history I did not trust any man. My sisters at this stage were very compassionate, as they had never seen me so upset.

Paddy Murphy used to visit on a regular basis. On his arrival, Father would give him a warm welcome and he always seemed to be in great form and very talkative. He was kind, and nice to children. Then, after about four days, his mood would change, and he would go into a black depression, not speaking to anyone and not eating. He always looked ill and it was surprising that no one ever suggested that he should see a doctor but depression was something that no one ever talked about in those days. No one went to a doctor, anyway, unless they were really ill. After about two weeks, he would leave and look for work close by. He liked to remain in the one area for a few months.

Those men had no way of travelling except by foot; it was amazing how they got around, as some used travel from county to county. They were very knowledgeable about the countryside and used to travel through the fields, taking shortcuts. They might arrive at the farm at any hour of the day or night.

Joe and Mick arrived at the farm one night very late, having travelled from Kerry. They were both chronic alcoholics, very shabbily dressed, and my father felt great compassion for them when he looked at their shoes. When they saw my father look at their shoes, they said,

'Never mind sir, when we are walking through the poodles of water, the water can go in one side and out the other'. They drank all their wages.

Mother liked them as they were jolly, and loved to sing. Mother was very musical, so she always liked people who could sing, was a very good violinist herself and could play most musical instruments. She could listen to Irish traditional music forever. I had no ear for music, but I loved dancing. If Mother were in a bad mood, she would take out the violin, or the fiddle as she used to call it, and then, as she started to play, her mood would change instantly. She also played the melodeon, or gadget as it was called, and taught some of the neighbours how to play.

Country life in those days was completely different to what it is today. We had no television, until 1960. All we had was the radio that we called the wireless. The wireless was old, and it was only switched on for the news, or if there was any traditional Irish music and then Mother would listen to it.

HARVEST TIME

I loved harvest time, as I loved corn; the warm golden colour always filled me with joy. At harvest time Father would get extra help. In those days farmers would help one another; money was never mentioned. If they saw a neighbour in difficulty because of bad weather, or health problems, they immediately went to his rescue.

I loved the excitement of the thrashing. This happened in the fall of the year. The corn was first cut, with a binder and horses, then gathered and put into sheaves. About eight sheaves were put standing on a cut edge, and this was called a stook. Then, after about a week, all the sheaves were brought into the farmyard. This part of the farmyard was called the haggard. Then the corn was put into big reeks, all ready for thrashing.

The steam engine came into the haggard the night before; it was like a touch of heaven, to hear the sound of the engine. I loved the day of the thrashing. It was a great social occasion and the women in the neighbourhood helped with the cooking. Mother had to get up early in the morning and the dinner always consisted of boiled bacon,
cabbage and potatoes. Pig heads and spare ribs were also used. A barrel of Guinness would arrive in the evening and, when it was dark and the work was finished, the men would come into the kitchen, and sit down and relax and everyone would drink as much porter as they wished. After supper mother would play music on the fiddle, and then look for someone to play the melodeon.

Then the ' Thrashing ball' would start! The ball consisted of dancing around the kitchen, on the concrete floor. When some of the men spilled porter on the floor, because they were drunk, we had to watch out in case we skidded or fell. When the men were drunk, or as they used to say' half soft', they would start to sing, usually ballads. The ball might go on until the small hours of the morning and arranged marriages were often made on those nights. Young women would come at night, offering to help make tea, but they really came to enjoy themselves and look for future husbands.

A Hound That Brought Me To The Ground

One day, when I was eleven years old, my mother sent me to a neighbour's house, to borrow some sugar. In those days, it was normal practice to call to your neighbour if you ran out of tea, or sugar. People at that time normally only shopped once a week.

As I approached the house, I saw this great, big dog coming towards me. I was terrified. He grabbed my leg and I thought he would never let me go. What kept going around in my mind was that my life was now over. This dog was so vicious; I was numb with shock. I did not even feel his sharp teeth enter my leg but, when I looked down, I saw blood pouring out. I was horrified, as I never liked the look of blood. I felt dizzy and thought that I was going to collapse with shock.

Inside I tried to be calm, and kept repeating the word 'calm'. I had nothing to hold on to. I was standing on one leg while the other one was being torn. It seemed like hours but was it only minutes? The dog finally opened his mouth and let go. I looked at him, and he looked at me with horrifying, bulging eyes. I just asked myself 'What satisfaction did he get by biting me?' I thought that he would go for some other part of me. I knew that I was in danger. Just then the owner of the dog came, and he immediately brought me home.

I told mother and father what had happened to me and Mother bandaged my leg so I thought I would be ok. She never took me to the doctor, or hospital. I trusted, mother knew best. I was not worried about scars on my legs, but the fear of dogs, and the barking of dogs. Was it the terror coming back to me? Mother treated me with bread and water poultices and some-times the poultices were very hot and caused me great pain. After one week, I became very sick but I thought it was shock. Mother realised that the wound was infected and Father took me to the hospital where I had to stay for three weeks. I had to have surgery on the wound as I ended up getting septicaemia (blood poisoning). I was very ill, but the staff in the hospital were very kind.

Nobody highlighted to me what long-term effects this bite could have on me. All my life, that terrifying look on that dog's face never left me. I have been terrified of dogs ever since. But now I use the name of Jesus, whenever I meet a vicious dog. I say in the name of Jesus be gone.

BITTEN BY A DOG

I crossed, the road, and on the other side was a green field.
I saw a dog he terrified me, and to him did I yield,
His grinning teeth stopped me on my tracks,
I thought by him my body would be axed.
Closer and closer he came, I was terrorised,
I wanted to scream, from looking at his size,
If I ran I knew he would follow,
Or that I would be torn by briars, and fall into a hollow.
None to turn to and no place to run,
To my head it was like a gun,
I was not ready, or prepared for the shot.
Was this my time place or plot?
I looked into his eyes, there was an evil glaze.
I thought if I petted him, this horror would be erased.
Fear held me back, I was in doubt.
God made such beautiful creatures with love,
Definitely this dog was possessed and not from above.
He eagerly waited for me to move,
I stood still, I had a point to prove.
Even if I was bitten, broken or damaged,
I had the strength, and attitude to get on and manage.
He grabbed me, and I felt I was tossed in the air,
My body went into shock, into his eyes I stared,

After what seemed like hours, I was finally let go,
I felt it was the final hour, when the cock crowed.
This scar in my memory still lives on,
And the scars on my legs, I know will never be gone.
Ever since that evil atrocity, I have a fear of dogs.
You never know when they will jump just like frogs.
But now I have words that are more convincing
In Jesus name be gone, is my defending.
I do not work alone, because Jesus is my rock,
If dogs gather around me like a flock.
In their pride they have turned and gone away.
Because, in the name of Jesus, I have had my say.
Evil in any creature never again, will come my way,
With the power of Jesus every animal will obey

My School Years

When I had finished my primary education in a small country school, I decided, with a little push from Mother, that I wanted to go to a boarding school. I thought that this would be a great escape from Mother's anger and the hardship I endured. Full of excitement I was packing my bags for weeks. I knew I would miss Father but I thought I would have the best of both worlds if I left. I would no longer have to listen to Mother roaring and shouting in my ears. 'Freedom!' I shouted, 'Freedom is my destiny!' The prison cell was open. I had read stories about how girls in England went to boarding schools and the life in these places seemed so exciting I could not wait to get there. I was always an avid reader and was fascinated by books. I could get lost for hours in any bookshop. My son John inherited this love for books and also one of my grandsons.

When I arrived at the boarding school Sr. Baptist showed me around. She gave me a very warm welcome and said, ' you'll enjoy your time here with us'. She was a nice woman and I always got on well with her. But when the rules were given to me I felt a bit freaky about them. All of a sudden I became scared. I wasn't liberated in the way I had thought I would be. It suddenly dawned on me that I was going from the frying pan into the fire and by God I felt it. When I entered the dormitories and saw the long row of beds on each side, it looked very strange to me, and the sister said ' No talking aloud in here after 9pm.'

Suddenly I was living in a room with other girls and instead of looking at them I looked inwards; I started to think more deeply and did not sense what was going on around me. These girls were not very friendly. Most of them came from very rich families, were utter snobs, and showed it. They used to look me up and down, from head to toe, and their stares made me feel very inferior. Even the girls that were not rich soon followed suit. They thought that they were important because they were boarders. Boarding schools in those days were designed to make you a lady and take the rough corners off your character. Some girls enjoyed it, but to me it was a prison cell.

There were other girls in the school, the 'day girls' and the poor orphans. The orphans' lives were very hard as they had to work long hours and never seemed to have any visitors or breaks. We were not allowed to mix with either group but I would have much preferred to be associated with those girls than the snobs. Some of the orphans suffered endlessly and I longed to talk to them, but I knew if I did, I would be in trouble. This class distinction really upset me. If I met an orphan on the stairs she would have to run to the bottom, put her head down and wait for the 'Lady' to go down first. I wondered how this could be Christian charity? Sitting with those girls and the 'day girls' in class, you could always tell who were the nuns' pets. Of course it was the boarders as they were rich, and they were always treated with respect and dignity. I only went home for school holidays and the odd weekend and always envied the 'day girls', as they could go home after school. I loved the school; it was staying there at night that I hated. I thought that it was an unnatural set-up and always longed for freedom.

The school was very much orientated towards sport. If you were good at sport you were popular with the nuns and I was about the worst in the school at sport as I found it very boring. This was another burden that I had to carry, as sport was compulsory. I loved gym but we did not have it very often. Mother insisted that I learn music, as she was a very good violinist but I have'nt a very good ear for music and found the piano uninteresting. I had had enough of the violin at home from listening to Mother.

I craved for my Father's company but I was glad to see the back of Mother. However, don't you worry, I had a nun, Sr. Rita, to take her place. I would have given her the personality of the year award. She was the 'person' all right but the 'ality' was in her attitude. Nothing was ever right and every word from her mouth was a bite. Looking into her eyes was like a death sentence because one glimpse of the evil there gave me nightmares. I put it down to the total evil of a person who loved authority. If you did not get all your homework right you had to kneel on the floor in front of her, give an excuse, and say you were sorry. I often said to myself that she should live with Mother for a week and see how they got on. I doubt if they ever would, as each would want to show the other who was boss.

Anyway, this nun was part of my life throughout secondary school. One day my youngest sister came to visit me and when she got back home she told Mother I looked very ill. Mother came to collect me and took me out of school for a few weeks. Mother was kind to me during this period. I had become ill from fear as I always did when I was a child and this fear never left me.

The nun in charge of the school was very angry with my Mother when she came to collect me and said 'Why didn't she tell us she was ill?' I stood up for myself for once, as I was no longer a child and said that I had told Sr. Rita and she had said I was 'shamming'. Sr. Rita's attitude then changed completely towards me, as she knew I was no longer a fool. She knew she could not keep me down any longer as I was growing into an adult. From then on, until I finished school, she was very tolerant and even at times went out of her way to be kind. I think it was from guilt as, when I returned after being ill, all the sisters could see that I had lost so much weight. The day that I left that boarding school was my liberation.

School was sometimes a break for me, to get away from my Mother, for when the holidays came I was treated like a slave, only there to fulfil her dreams and wishes.

THE BEAMING TOUCH OF GOD

All my life I felt close to God, because I never had anyone, bar my Dad, to turn to and he was afraid at times because he did not want to upset Mother. Throughout my suffering as a child, I would always weep and feel a hand close to me; it was the hand of God that was so tender. God knew of my suffering and he understood, but I could never understand why he let it continue.

When I was preparing for my confirmation, I was learning, 'The life of our Lord', from a miniature bible and I was very interested in the parables and miracles that Jesus had performed. Then, one day, I picked up a Catholic magazine, 'The messenger of the Sacred Heart' and as I read it I came to know of Jesus and the power of His love if I trusted in Him. I read of answered requests so I started to pray in a deeper way and invited Jesus into my life. I asked Him to help me to cope with all the mundane things of everyday life because, being so full of fear made every day a struggle.

I have many fears that go back to my childhood; they haunt me and sometimes make me very depressed because although I have got over some of them, others still affect me. I have a terrible fear of water and I suffered as a child from a fear of horses. My father was a very gentle, kind and peaceful man. When he was a young boy, a horse threw him to the ground and as a result he suffered from a back injury for years. In later life he was a bit harsh with horses, as he never again wanted them to control him.

One of my greatest fears, even now, is of men. Brian was the only one that overcame that; I think that was because of his wonderful qualities of gentleness and kindness. I am still afraid of water, even walking beside a river or over a bridge it is as if I have been deposited into the river. Whatever happened to me as a child regarding water, it must have happened before I became aware of my mother's cruelty because my Mother did not just become cruel all of a sudden.

I never realised I was so afraid of water until I went to Garnish Island, a little island off Glengarrif on the south- west coast of Ireland. About 30 years ago a group of friends and myself went on a small motorboat across to the Island. It took about half an hour to cross and when I was just half way over, I panicked and wanted to jump into the water, because I felt I could not go any further. My friends could not understand why I was afraid. They did their best to calm me down but when I got off the boat I collapsed and one of my friends, Mona, had to get a glass of brandy to revive me. When I knew I was no longer in the water I got over it, but the memory of it still lingers on.

People also frighten me, not by their moods or looks, but just people in general, particularly those in authority. In my childhood I was terrified of schoolteachers and when I was nursing I had an unnatural fear of the matron. Sometimes even my own shadow scares me. Fear itself is more a part of my life than of any others. Expelling my fear is a virtue, because then God can take control, but some of my fears I cannot expel, as they are too severe. Layer by layer, Jesus is healing them and moment by moment as they are lifted, it is like a new breath of fresh air. There are 2 kinds of fear, the awesome fear of God and the fear of the devil. Jesus said 365 times in the bible, ' do not be afraid'. My motto now in life is, ' face the fear and do it anyway', and then God will have His say.

My fears as a child

As you can see from my mother I
Suffered from fear,
My mind from torture was never clear
Down my face my painful tears,
Every little word was ringing in my ears.
Repeating those nasty words I could not take,
It was just like another flake,
The agony was so excruciating and so hard,
I felt I had no adult near me to guard,
In my fields of corn many times I dazed,
Of a wonderful mother in sight I would glaze.
My life was more than a hazy sunshine,
So many different combinations to combine,
In my heart I an angry mother's
Impression,
About everything I had to use my own discretion,
Sooner or later I had to grow up and be smart,
Because in my life my mother had no special part,
She caused me a lot of pain which I
Endured,
And into her manipulation, I no longer
Wanted to be lured,
A mother of love, peace and kindness should have hailed,
But unfortunately in my life she had failed.

A Heavenly Experience with Our Lady

I had now become seven and this was the year that I was to make my first Holy Communion. I was looking forward to it, as I had heard other children talk about what a lovely day they had had. I was thinking ahead to a beautiful family gathering, because I never used to experience this fulfilment. It so often happened in my life that, when relations called, I would be put out of the room. I thought that for once this would be my day, and that mother would look at me proudly. Two other boys prepared for Holy Communion with me and I was very nervous, as Miss Lynch, the schoolteacher preparing me, was so bad-tempered. Nan helped me with my catechism and my prayers. She was so kind, and she had great patience. Mother never helped me in any way.

I wore a lovely white dress and white veil, and I carried a bouquet of flowers. Miss Hussey, who lived in the village nearby, had a lovely garden, and she gave me the flowers. I walked proudly up the aisle to the seat where Miss Lynch was sitting. To my bitter disappointment the boys never turned up due to a last minute illness and I was left all alone with her. I was so terrified of her that I felt sick, and could hardly pray. I looked up at the priest and he had a kind face but Mother was in a seat close by and I was afraid that if I made any mistakes Mother would have an excuse to turn on me. It was most unusual at that time, because the little school had always had six or seven children every year for Communion. When I had received Holy Communion I prayed to Jesus, for Miss Lynch, Mother, Nan and all my family, who had prepared me for this wonderful day, but when I went home, to my disappointment it was just like any other.

All my life I had a great love for Our Lady. I knew that I had a connection with her. I always dreamed about her and how beautiful she looked. I wished that I had a life of happiness like her, not knowing back then that her son Jesus was crucified. She was my Heavenly Mother and I wished she could come down and enfold me in her motherly love. What good was a picture or a statue? They could not help me. I noticed from a very young age that Our Lady's eyes would follow me from a statue or a picture. I dreamed of Angels, That I too was flying among them and that they were directing and guiding me. One of my Angels was named Charlie and the other Philip. I believed as a child that if I called them by their names, thy would come to me.

These dreams are known in spiritual terms as mystical dreams. One night I had a very important vision in my sleep. This was clearer and more vivid than the other dreams. It was a dream where God revealed to me, that he had a special plan for me and for my life. There were numerous occasions, when I heard God calling me. Being a child I did not take much interest, as I was caught up in a world of suffering. God kept telling me in different ways, that He would 'bake my bread and I would rise and shine'. He told me I would not any longer be the dough, that other people kept kneading. He would transform me into a beautiful bread.

When I was 12 years of age I went for a walk to my favourite place in the well field, and as I stood still for a moment Our lady spoke to my heart; this is called a locution. She gave me a very powerful message concerning the Holy Souls (souls who have died, but not yet gone to Heaven) and I could feel both their pain and their need of prayer and a great sadness came over me. Then Our Lady told me to pray a lot of rosaries for them and I promised Her that I would, especially when I was older. From then on, to the present day, I became very close to Our Lady but, for some reason, I never shared this awesome experience with anyone.

In 1991 I visited a church and I was just beginning to pray when all of a sudden I had a vision. I saw a large group of people facing me, instead of the altar; they were all of different nationalities and some of them were dressed in very strange clothes. Some of them looked Spanish and I could see an Indian with a very red face and long black hair. I knew none of them and they were all starting to stare at me. Their very stare seemed to penetrate my soul. A beautiful young girl, who was about 13 years old, stood in front of me, very smartly dressed. The vision changed and some of them appeared in framed pictures and the Indian appeared as a statue. It was revealed to me that they were all Holy souls searching for prayer. The Holy Souls now appear to me on a regular basis seeking my prayers, so you can see it is very important to pray for our loved ones who have passed away because our prayers can shorten their purgatory and help them get to heaven sooner. Indulgences, also, which we do not hear much about nowadays are a powerful means of help to them. It is very important to have masses said and visit the cemetery and pray at the graves of our loved ones. Cemeteries should be treated with great respect, as they are consecrated grounds.

THE STATIONS

The Stations were a great social occasion in the country, when I was growing up. They originated from 'The Penal Times', when catholic churches were closed and monasteries were burned. The priests who 'were on the run' used to say mass by the sea, amongst the rocks, which became called mass rocks, or in houses at night.

We had the Station, when mass would be said, about every five years in our house and the preparations would start months before. The house would be completely cleaned but, as Mother was a very domesticated and organised person, she never made much of a fuss about having the Station. All the neighbours would come and my parents thought it was a great privilege to have mass said in our house.

Father was very different to Mother and broken pillars and gates that had lost their balance never worried him, but to please Mother all broken walls were repaired, and gates that had sagged previously, now swung freely. You could open and close them properly, instead of having to move a big stone every time you went through, and loose galvanised sheeting was made secure. All the outhouses were whitewashed with a mixture of lime and water and all the doors were painted black; I think they used tar.

On the night before the Station it was usually very busy. Tables were set in the parlour with the best china, and bowls of lump sugar and dishes of butter rolls were then put on the table while the fires were laid for the next day. The altar would be set on the kitchen table and covered with a special white sheet, which was only used for Stations or Wakes. In the 1940's, sheets for everyday use were made out of empty flour bags that were bleached and then sown together; about four bags would be sufficient for one sheet and tea towels and pillowcases were also made out of flour bags. But on Station day this special sheet was used and on top of that would be laid the best lace cloth and then two brass candlesticks and a crucifix.

On that morning everyone got up early, but Father in particular, as he had to do the milking. Then, when he was dressed up in his best suit, his job was to welcome the priests and neighbours at the front door. When the priests arrived, one would hear confessions in the parlour, while the other put on his vestments to prepare for mass, and, after mass dues were collected, the priests took names for the next Station. I always got a nice warm feeling when mass was said in the house.

After mass, the Station breakfast of tea, boiled eggs, brown bread currant brack, and apple tarts was served. The priests had toast, which was toasted on the fire, by holding the bread with a fork.

Neighbours who could not come in the morning came in the afternoon and relatives such as aunts and uncles could arrive at any time as the Station sometimes continued into the night. The priests usually left after breakfast and then the whiskey and bottles of Guinness were served, together with port wine for the women and white lemonade, `Little Nora`, for the children. Everyone would sit around, relaxed, as we had a fire in the kitchen, and one in the parlour. The fire in the parlour was hardly ever light, other than at Station times, and it gave the room a nice warm look.

THE STATIONS

The Stations were an important feature in everyone's life,
They all took it in turn, to make goodness strive.
Meeting with neighbours on this occasion brought them together,
So that no one was left alone to wither.
In those times loneliness was less,
Neighbours were all invited in as guests.
Everyone took his turn to have the station mass.
Society was humble, with no upper class,
The rich and the poor were a symbol of peace,
And with their love, their faith increased.
People were human, not like today,
Materialism is God and has its say.
The Station Mass was like the last supper,
Love, peace and joy in gathering did always occur.
It was also a chance for those alone in their community, to feel at home.
The people would gather, the priest would arrive,
With such a feeling of awe it was great to be alive.
As we said the prayers the Mass would proceed,
Afterwards all would celebrate with a great feed
We were so happy together and as a community united.
Those days are long gone, when one looked after another.
When everyone were like brother and sister.
There is always happiness when God is in our midst.
In God's work, love always fits.

BIG DAN'S STATION

When Dan's turn came up to have the station, the priest said: "You have nice daffodils growing on the ditch near your house". Dan's reply was: "You need more than daffodils to have a station."

Dan's station was different to any other station, because a lot of work had to be done. Dan lived with his two brothers and two sisters who were all good at farm work, but Josie and Elley were not cut out for housework. The house was full of mice and maybe an occasional rat. Cats and dogs also lived in the house and if pigs and sheep were sick, they were nursed back to health in the parlour. Young chicks were kept in the kitchen, until they were six weeks old. So you can imagine the work that had to be done in this house for the station. They had to start to prepare a year in advance and Josie complained constantly about the preparations and decoration.

If it hadn't been for the neighbours helping, Dan would never have had the station at all. All the local women got together and started cleaning. The rafters were black, from the smoke of the open fire and had to be white-washed and the concrete floors had to be scrubbed, as they were filthy from the animals. Josie was warned to keep all the animals out until after the station. Theresa, who lived nest door, tried to clean the clevy (the shelf over the open fire) and this shelf had never been cleaned from one station to another. It was full of cobwebs and while she was cleaning it out popped a brown mouse. She screamed with fright and Josie could not understand what all the fuss was about.

The night before the station was hilarious. Dan never bothered to paint the outhouses, but he painted the front of the farmhouse, and cleaned the entrance. Elley baked two big current cakes in the bastable. The bastable was an oven used over an open fire. She put a cross on each cake, which was the custom at that time To her the cross represented the cross of Christ. Then the women set the tables for breakfast.

When the priests came on the morning of the station, Dan gave them a warm welcome. Towards the end of the Mass, just after Holy Communion, I thought the priest was going to fall over, but when I looked again, I saw a big sheepdog caught in the priest's vestments. The dog freed himself, and everyone laughed but Josie lost her temper and blamed Denny (another brother) for not locking the dog up. Denny said that the dog must have opened the door himself. Josie could not see the funny side of it – she just felt very embarrassed in front of her neighbours. Her face was red as a beetroot as she shouted shrilly at Denny.

Breakfast was then served; cups were taken off the dresser and everyone got his or her tea, current cake and eggs. After breakfast everyone went away home and Dan and the rest of the family were glad to see the back of them. They did not like too many people about and apart from that they were afraid that some nosy person might go upstairs and see the hens laying eggs!

On the evening of Dan's station. Denny complained of a pain in his chest. The family warned him not to tell anyone because sickness was considered a sign of weakness, and compassion for illness did not exist. They decided not to call the doctor in case the neighbours should see the car coming up the drive. In that time only the doctor, the parish priest, or a very wealthy farmer owned a car.

Within the next hour a man came to the house looking for cattle which had strayed from his farm. He gave Denny one glance before telling them to get a doctor and an ambulance or they would live to regret it. After taking his advice Danny was admitted to hospital with acute bronchitis.

One of the first things they did was to help Denny have a bath, which was enough to give him a heart attack in itself because he only ever washed his face on a Sunday morning and his feet a couple of times a year. Then the nurses found an old pair of pyjamas that had belonged to someone who had passed away and put them on. At this point Denny became angry and said he wanted to wear his waistcoat on top of his pyjamas. On making a list of his personal belongings, they discovered two thousand pounds hidden in his waistcoat. In those days that money would have bought a seventy-acre farm. When the nurse told him she would keep it safe in the Nurse's Office, Denny would not hear of it and said: "I minded it all my life and I will continue to mind it until the last nail is driven into my coffin."

Denny found hospital life very strange, particularly as he could not cope with all the hygiene. After about four weeks he was discharged and warned to take life easy as he had a weak heart but as soon as he arrived home the family told him to get back into the work routine on the farm.

In those days farmers fought over "boundary" ditches" - the ditches dividing one field from another. It was up to each farmer to fence their side properly so that cattle would not stray from one farm to another but some owners were careless and if their animals strayed on to fields of corn or barley all hell broke loose. Farmers would fight and then sometimes remain enemies for up to ten years, forbidding their children to talk to the neighbour's kids as well.

One day Denny saw some strange cattle on his land, he realised whose cattle they were and saw a gap in the boundary ditch. When he went to the owner they both decided to fence the ditch in such a way as to prevent a reoccurrence. Normally Denny would have been very angry but the hospital episode had a mellowing effect on his spirit. It was as if he had returned from a foreign country where he had seen how different people lived: - the boundary no longer seemed such a big thing.

After he had been home for a short while Denny complained of a severe pain in his chest. As Josie had already cooked the dinner she made him eat some food and then told him to go to bed and have a lie down. When she went to call him for his tea, he was dead. Then she notified the priest, to give him the last rites.

Then all the fuss started, as they had to prepare for "The Wake". A wake was a major event in Ireland. Neighbours were notified and as nobody ever went upstairs in this house except for the family, the hens and the dogs. Denny's room was cleaned and scrubbed from top to bottom they used disinfectant to take the smell of the animals out of the room. Then they borrowed white linen sheets which were only used for special occasions as alter cloths and as sheets for the wake bed. They borrowed them from Molly next door who had received hers in the traditional manner, as a wedding present.. After scrubbing down the bedroom floor they put the hens and dogs in the outhouse.

In that time men were laid out in brown habits that were sold in drapers' shops and were put on the deceased person after being blessed by the priest. Some people bought these ten years in advance to be in readiness for the wake. I personally thought the habit was morbid.

Dan went off to get a good supply of whiskey and beer and some port wine for the ladies. Cooked ham was bought and loaves of "shop bread", so called because people always baked their own bread. In the "waking" room there was usually a table beside the bed where seven candles were lit, with a crucifix in the centre and holy water. Pictures and mirrors were covered. Some folk stayed with the corpse all the time, either praying or just remaining silent.

Denny's Wake went on all day and late into the evening. Ted, who lived down the boreen, said he would relieve some of the women who sat by the corpse, but as he had drank a lot, he forgot, after a while, where he was and started to sing "Bantry Bay". Poor Josie and Elley nearly passed away, themselves when they heard him singing! They thought it was very disrespectful but all the neighbours laughed as they could see the humourous side of it. I just wondered whether there was a "banshee" in the room (a banshee was a mourning spirit that In Irish tradition was supposed to come at the time of death.).

As the relatives, neighbours and friends arrived they sympathised with the family and when my Father said: "Dan I'm sorry for your trouble," Dan's reply was: "he never gave me trouble – he ate his dinner then went upstairs and died."

A wake was very expensive for poor families but relatives usually helped out. After two days Denny was laid to rest. Whiskey was given out in the graveyard, which was the custom at that time.

My Teenage Years

As I grew older I became more aware of how my Mother and I clashed. As a child my cornfields were my freedom, but as a teenager I was bored. I had the odd boyfriend but nothing serious; as I have said before I was afraid of men. I was afraid of everyone. I became empty and depressed as a teenager because my house was like a battlefield; I felt so inferior to my sisters. Inside myself I was torn apart. My Mother made me feel so inadequate that on the outside I was protecting myself from an endless war. As you know, one thing we are given as children, from our parents, are set ideas and set ways, and we follow them whether they good or bad. They grow inside us like a tree and that's what happened with my sisters; they had certain beliefs and followed them faithfully and the cost was that I was hurt. Mother's ways with me rubbed off on them. As a teenager I never felt worthy because I became more aware of my eyesight impairment, and the more I thought about it the more it became a problem. I thought no one would fancy me and I asked myself what was the point in living when everyone around me was perfect. The clothes I wore were very different to other peoples;. As I became older I began to choose my own fashion and that gave me more confidence.

Time moved on and I no longer looked up to my Mother because I knew what she was really like. I learned from this stage on never to take anything she said seriously. From a young age my Mother had emotionally traumatised me, which is the worst and most severe type of pain. I became so used to it that if I had a physical pain I wouldn't feel it because my body would shut down and go numb.

I had to learn how to feel and express myself properly and it took some time to get it right. I had to break the chains and take down the barriers that caused me to be different because of my upbringing. I often wondered why I had different thoughts to other people, the greatest gifts God gave to me were to understand myself, to be patient, and not to be so hard on myself. When there is a part of us fractured in life we must take good care of ourselves. It's important that we do not live too hard or expect too much of ourselves. Loving ourselves is just a soothing healing that we need to experience.

Trusting in God

There were many old ways in my life that I did not show, especially my suffering and how I felt. It was as if I had a cap on my head, covering my face; it was an unrealistic description. Thanks be to God, I had Father when he came up from the farm. God is love and truth, but I saw no truth in suffering. He said that He carried me, but what did he mean by this, when my suffering was endless. My life goes on with memories that even today still unfold. Healing is a gradual process; you must expel painful memories one by one, not like a computer that downloads everything at once.

Trusting in God was my only hope, whether I thought He existed or not. Where else do you put your hope when you see no light. My only light was my belief. The mind is a very powerful weapon; it can lift you up, or lower you down. Jesus has changed me from a stone that was still, to a stone that He uses to build a house.

Everyone feels anger towards God, even me. We do not understand His ways, because of our limited intelligence. If God were to give man any more than he has, he would try and control God. As you can already see, he is trying to do it in different ways, but he will fall and crumble.

All my life, I have tried to cross the river, whether it was by rafts, barrels or whatever but I never reached the other side until I was fifty years old. I knew God by now, and I knew He was powerful. I was not His vessel when I floated across the river from side to side but I am now his vessel, and I carry God's people from the water banks, where they have nearly drowned, to the dry banks on the other side.

Every person that turns to God has a role, because God chooses him to do His work. The work is to let other people know the truth about God, and the need for conversion in the world. Just as in a food chain, everyone then would know about God. We can all reach out in the love of God, because it enlightens our hearts.

Running With Nature

When I was a child, how I loved to run and run and try to enjoy the fun. It was like floating on air, not thinking of where I put each foot but only to keep on running. I used to love to hide and try not to be caught, holding my breath in case my breathing was heard. Sitting in the grass without a care or worry I enjoyed my own company. Dogs were the best playthings of all and I used to love running with them. There was no cheek, and no answering back. My fun time would not last long, because you know about my hard life and my duties, but I used to love counting the fields, and sneaking into different gaps. Still, I was afraid I would be caught.

I loved the cows, but at times I was afraid of them. I was fascinated about looking at them and could never understand why they were chewing all the time. I thought when they ate grass that it was gone. I always thought that they were intelligent animals, because before it rained they would lie down, and I could hear the crows in the trees making a noise and I thought that that was another reason to think that rain was not far away.

I was in love with nature, and fascinated by it. I used to love picking wild flowers, making daisy chains and putting them around my neck. The freedom to run around was good for me. It was not so good when nettles and thistles stung me! I used to love to walk in the bog and pick rushes, and then make baskets out of them. I also made plaits, and canes. I thought that I was so clever.

We used to have a lot of small wells on our farm, where water used to run. I thought they were wishing wells. Some people used to put money into the wells and make a wish. As people had no running water in their homes in those times, as many as three or four different households would draw water from the same well. Our well was a meeting place for some of the women who drew water. The water from the well was ice cold and, when I heard the water running it gave me a great sense of peace.

I hated trespassing on other people's land, but it was also fun. In ditches overgrown with briars and wild grass, I might see a rusty plough and used to get a stick to break away the briars and have a good look. I would then make up a story, and imagine a horse pulling the plough, up and down the field. Then in my mind I would see a flock of seagulls, coming to eat the worms as the field was being ploughed. As I turned around, I might see rabbits running about playing. They were very numerous in those days and were a nuisance to farmers, as they ate a lot of their crops. I used to love climbing trees to see birds` nests and hear the little chickens chirping but was afraid to go too near in case the mother bird pecked me. I was always fascinated by the perfect way the nests were made. I was like a little kid from the Wild West, because I lived so close to nature.

I used to love to see castles and old ruins and pretend that I lived in that era. I imagined that I was rich, and wore beautiful clothes. My ideas would soon change, when I smelt the cows! I loved old dirt tracks, and I often saw cows walking on them. I used to take off my wellingtons, and walk on my bare feet on the dirt track. For some reason, this gave me a sense of freedom, and, with a stick in my hand, I felt important. I would knock down nettles and thistles, as I walked on. Inside I felt down, but outside I was happy. Living inside my house was like being in a dungeon. Being free made me excitable, as if I was a dog that wanted to go out for a run, but I might be as far as ten fields away, and Mother's loud voice could still be heard.

Some of the hens that were old used to wander away from the farmyard into the fields. Their cackling noise was different to younger hens and I used to love listening to them, thinking that they were singing because they were happy and free. I loved to see the pheasants too, with their beautiful colours; we found them regularly in the cornfields.

I used to love picking wild blackberries, strawberries, raspberries and sloes, and climbing the crab apple trees, and plum trees, which were growing wild on the farm. I used to eat a lot of the plums, as they were smaller and sweeter than the garden ones.

The nicest time of the year for me was August though, when the corn was being cut. I used to watch my father, as he cut the corn with three horses and a binder. When the corn was put into sheaves, I used sit on top of the sheaves of corn. It felt like a nice bed of gold and I often stole some and gave it to the cows. I picked branches off the trees too and fed the cows with them. I tried to keep myself happy despite all I went through but I still felt it would have been nicer to share these happy experiences with another child, instead of always being on my own.

THE TENDER MOMENT THAT TURNED
TO SPLENDOUR

Father used to carry large amount of vegetables, from the farm to the farmyard in a horse and cart. The vegetables were turnips, mangles and potatoes. The turnips were chopped up into small pieces in a large turnip machine, and then fed to the cattle. The potatoes were boiled and fed to the pigs. Pet used to feed the cattle, and care for them. Sometimes she would let me help her

Dad often took me for a spin in the horse and cart around the farm. I loved being with him and we sang together .Neither of us were able to sing, but our audience enjoyed us, the birds and the animals Father's favourite song was: "'If I were a blackbird , I'd whistle and sing and follow the boat that my true love sailed in ," I used to love to look up at the clear blue sky. I would think that the clouds were balls of cotton wool .for the Angels to float on.

Near the turnip field, Jack Hogan lived in a little house; every time I went with father to the turnip field I called into see Jack. He was a kind gentleman and had a profound humility. He enjoyed the simple things in life. Materialism never got to him. He lived in a little thatched cottage. He had his little eccentric ways – he never liked intruders at mealtimes. He would cover the windows with newspaper and lock the door when he sat down to table.

When I called to Jack's house, I knocked, then I shouted: "Eileen is here." I loved Jack's house, as I always felt peace in it. For a tablecloth he also used newspaper. His main diet, was goat's milk, cheese and fish. Sometimes he would exchange fish for mother's soda bread and eggs. He was a keen fisherman and a great friend of fathers.

He had a sister who immigrated to Boston and she used to send him home the "Boston Post" and some clothes. I used to read the comic section in the newspaper. This was great fun, as I never had comics at home. I then got interested in America, and how the people lived out there. Little did I think, back then that my sons would be living there in the future.

Jack told me a story that was in the newspaper, how a young child was kidnapped from a Boston family. An intruder broke into a house, snatched a child, from a babysitter at gunpoint. As I already said that my life was controlled by fear but after hearing Jack's story, I was afraid to go to bed at night. I could visualise someone coming in the window while I was asleep, who would then take me to the woods and feed me to the wild animals.

As I said previously, my house was like a prison, that is why it was lovely to relax and soak in the peace of Jack's house. My life was similar to the children who suffered in the orphanages, that is why I can understand their suffering. I have met some of them, and I could identify with them. Many suffer from mental illness. I told the children to come forward and tell their stories. I know that they too are broken. Some deaden their painful memories with alcohol.

They are very reluctant to tell me anything about experiences in the orphanages. It was like as if they put a lid on that part of their life. They did not want to lift the lid, in case the pain would be too severe. You could see suffering in their eyes, as they were not yet healed of their broken childhood.

They told me that the Christian Brothers and the nuns had their pets and that those children were well cared for. This made it more painful for the rest of the children who were not treated so kindly. I found that if you showed them any kind of love or kindness they found it difficult to accept. Like me, they were made feel unworthy to be loved.

Some were never called by their name. You can imagine how hurtful this must have been. As it says in scripture: "I have called you by your name, you are mine. " (Jeremiah) Praise God who watches over everything, who is infinite in love and infinite in justice. As it says in scripture "It would be better to have a stone put around your neck and thrown into the bottom of the sea than cause one of these little ones to sin."

THE HANDS OF THE LORD

The hands of the Lord have never failed me; even when I was down, he lifted me up. When I was up he held me. He walked down the path of suffering into the darkest places of my heart and gave me hope. This was the little bright light that kept me alive. It still shines through me but in a different brighter way now.

For years I felt I was down and broken and at the wayside. When I passed a river, I used to look into it and see a reflection. I thought this was an angel following me and for years I believed it. Angels are above and below, protecting us and they are always a step ahead warning us in case anything will happen. I know that my guardian angel has always been looking after me.

A New Horizon Opened Up For Me

When I was younger I did not have any choices and having no choices is like having no hands. Decisions help us to explore things and make us strong. They give us the self worth to be independent and make us confident people who are not afraid of taking chances. Decision -making means you are not afraid of the unknown future. It helps us to cope with uncertainty, to accept the failures and to enjoy the successes and has an important affect on the development of our personalities. As the saying goes, 'if you give yourself fears of decision making your mind will have its limits'. In effect, the only limitations on the development of your personality are those you impose yourself.

When I was a child I was not allowed to make such choices, not even the kind of toys I wanted to play with, what food I wanted or the clothes I would like to wear. Some people can make a hundred or even a thousand decisions in one day, others very few. I found it so hard to make any decision because I was not allowed to make any choices until I left home. The fear of failure, of my Mother's harsh criticism, completely deflated my confidence and self esteem.

When I left school I felt a tremendous sense of freedom as that part of my life was over. All I wanted to do now was to leave home, get a job, have my own money and be independent. I was undecided as to whether I would train to be a teacher or a nurse. I wanted to be a teacher as I have a great love for children and teachers were so unpleasant in our school when I was young, caning children for the least little thing. I thought, perhaps, I could do it differently. Then I opted for nursing as I always felt a deep sorrow for those who were sick. Knowing suffering as I did I could understand their pain and show them love and kindness. I always tried to be extra kind to the difficult patients as I felt they were hurting inside and some of the other nurses were hard on them.

Starting nursing was the best move I ever made and I enjoyed every minute of it. It was great to earn my own money even if my pay packet was small and a wonderful feeling to choose my own clothes for the first time in my life. In those days life was different for young people, the pace was slower, we had great fun and we laughed at nothing. It is hard for young people to understand that today. I made life-long friends in the girls that I trained with. We had great joy in our lives and although we worked hard, at the end of a long day when a patient would look up and say 'God bless you' that was all I needed, to know that nursing was my career. The hospital I trained in was a small Protestant hospital, as in those days you had either Catholic or Protestant hospitals. Nuns ran the Catholic ones and all the ward sisters were nuns whereas for the most part Protestant staff ran the others. All the doctors and ward sisters were Protestants. There was a lovely atmosphere in the one where I trained. We never had religious bigotry or class distinction; we were all equal as if we were one big happy family. As the hospital was small it was affiliated to a larger hospital in Dublin where we did our final year. Working there was in sharp contrast to the hospital I had left. Besides nursing we dusted and kept the wards clean, as well as having to sluice dirty laundry, as there were no disposable sheets in those days. Some of the ward sisters there were very harsh. One of them was very bitter and we used to call her hatchet face. She went out of her way to make life difficult for every nurse who worked under her. She used everyone as a corner stone for her anger. Perhaps life went wrong for her when she was young and she was a very unhappy woman. Some of the ward sisters had no social life and simply went from their work to their rooms, which were in the nurses' home adjoining the hospital. My friends and I had a wonderful social life, as Dublin was an exciting place for young people in the late fifties. We had the Theatre Royal, the Abbey and all the cinemas, as well as the dance halls. The hospitals were run very strictly in Dublin and we had to be home by 10 O' clock unless we had special leave. My nursing training was a help to me throughout my life.

In 1959 a lovely little girl called Lisa was admitted to the children's ward. She was 11 years old and diagnosed with T.B in her kidney. Lisa was a lovely, gentle little girl, very polite and well mannered. An only child, she settled down very quickly to the hospital routine. She never complained and she was always very pleasant and helpful to the other patients even offering to help me do little chores and make the beds. Her mother used to call to see her every day for the whole afternoon. After about 2 months she complained of a pain in her back but the doctor said she was just a spoilt child and that her mother was making a fuss, as she was her only child. I was told to simply give her an injection of sterile water every time she complained of pain. She used to ask me for her injection and I felt so sorry for her as she looked up into my face and said 'thank you very much nurse'. This went on for another 6 weeks. I became very close to Lisa and we became great friends. I could see that she was losing weight and then her colour changed and she looked very pale and ill. When the doctors finally did some x-rays and tests Lisa was diagnosed with cancer of the kidney, so you can imagine the pain she had been suffering. Her illness gradually progressed and she still never once complained but at least now she had painkillers in her injection.

God worked a miracle for her mother as the mother became pregnant and when Lisa heard the good news she was so happy. Little Lisa did not live to see her new sister. God took her to her eternal home in heaven where there is no more pain or tears. I know Lisa is a little saint in heaven singing songs of praise with all the other child saints.

We were called every morning at 6. 30.a.m. by an electric clock and I can still remember the sound. We had to be in our own dining hall for 7.15.a.m. and on the wards at 7.45.a.m. Hospital life was very different in those days because of class distinction; the surgeons and the doctors were treated as gods. The wards had to be immaculate prior to the doctor's rounds. Student nurses were their slaves and if they left needles or syringes around the nurses would have to clean up after them. Patients never dared to ask questions. The ward sisters played up to the doctors as I think they were afraid of them. I worked in Theatre as a student nurse in the 'ear , nose and throat` section. My first job when the surgeon arrived in Theatre was to open his cufflinks and put them in a safe place and if it was a warm day I had to get a facecloth and wipe his forehead. Then the ward sister used to keep smiling at the doctor all morning and I used to think that she fancied him as she showed a different face to me. She used say; 'if you make one mistake when you are scrubbed up I will kick you under the table'. Today it would be impossible to imagine a Ward Sister behaving like that but they were often jealous of the young nurses and gave them a very hard time. They were not always kind to patients either and were even overbearing to the visitors but behaved quite differently to private patients, as they knew they would not get away with any mistreatment. The Nurses, Domestic staff, or Maids as they were then called, and Doctors, all had separate dining halls and the Homes were similarly segregated.

I worked in casualty on night duty and as the hospital was in the city centre it was very convenient for the Dublin Fire Brigade ambulance and we were always run off our feet. We got a lot of our patients from the Fatima flats and Kevin street flats, which were very near the hospital. I remember one morning at 2.a.m. two old ladies in their sixties, Mary and Katie Ann, had a row outside Kevin street flats. They were both drunk so they started shouting and screaming and pulling each other`s hair out. Mary was the stronger of the two so she pulled nearly all the hair out of poor Katie Ann's head and clawed at her face with her nails. The guards from Kevin Street Garda station were sent for and these ladies, who were well known by the guards, were very abusive towards them. Katie Anne was sent to hospital by ambulance as blood was streaming down her face and when she arrived I sat her down and got a doctor to examine her. When I dressed her wounds she started using foul language and abusing me as if I had caused the damage! I put her lying on a couch in a cubicle on her own while I went off to see to another patient and the next thing I heard was ' The old triangle goes jingle jangle `. I told her to be quite as she was disturbing other patients. She said 'F....... Off you culchie and go back to the bogs', but when she realised I meant business she said, 'sorry, sorry, nurse', and she joined her hands and said, 'Suffering Jesus get me out of here'. Then she went off to sleep and she slept for 3 hours. When I noticed a little stream coming from her cubicle I wiped up the floor but dared not disturb her.

When she woke up I gave her a cup of tea and 2 Painkillers for her head. Then she joined her hands in prayer and said, 'Jesus, Mary and blessed Joseph take pity on me and take this brutal headache away'. She had sobered up considerably and then she walked home as the flats were close to the hospital. I never met Katie Ann again and I regularly walked by the block of flats.

Her friend Alice also lived in the same street opposite the flats. Alice had a little chipper. Her place was filthy and the floor looked as if it was never washed. The walls were also dirty looking. Alice herself looked very untidy but she was very warm and friendly and always seemed to be in good form. I never tasted chips as nice as the ones in Alice's chipper. For 6d you got a fine lot of chips wrapped up in a couple of sheets of newspaper so as well as eating your chips you could have a read of the Evening Mail or the Herald. There were 2-second hand shops further up the street. I often went into one and Molly would give you a few bob for clothes. Molly always looked very posh. She had her blonde hair in a beehive style and she said ' I never comb it in between my visits to the hair dresser'. It was absolutely covered with hair spray. She wore bright red lipstick and gold earrings and she always wore black. She always loved black clothes and paid more money when you brought them. She said she used to travel to the country fairs and they sold better. My friend from Galway used to get black clothes from relatives in America and we would take them down to Molly to get the price of the pictures (Cinema). Molly used to love to chat and I was always amused passing her shop, because, 5 minutes after giving her the clothes you could see them displayed in her shop window.

Dublin was full of characters in those days. Ned was a great friend of mine and a regular patient in the hospital as he was a bad asthmatic. When I was on night duty he was always looking for cups of tea. When I look back I think he was addicted to tea. He seemed to sleep very little at night. We were not allowed to give tea after 9 p.m. but Ned was so persistent I often broke the rules and gave him tea at all hours. When I was busy he used to make it himself from the hot tap in the ward. He watched out for me in case I got into trouble with the night sister. When Ned was discharged he used to call in to see me, looking for the clothes and hats of people who had passed away. If the relations did not collect the clothes I kept them for Ned. He smoked asthmatic cigarettes and the very smell of them used to drive the other patients crazy.

Danny was a porter in the hospital and one of his jobs was to light the fires in the wards. In those days you had open fires in the large wards. Every floor in the hospital had one big ward with about 30 beds, 15 on either side. As student nurses we had to help with cleaning the bathroom and dusting the wards. Danny was a very pompous character. He was only about 5 foot 3 inches tall but he walked around as if he owned the hospital. He was about 50 years old and spent his time trying to get the attention of the domestic staff. Danny really fancied himself and thought he was God's gift to women. He was admitted as a patient to St Brendan's - that was the ward I worked in - and when I was admitting him he looked up at me and he said very proudly, ' I have syphilis Miss'. He had no idea what it meant. He just heard the doctor saying it. I thought at the time it was hilarious.

Although we had great fun socialising we had very small pay packets, with the result that we had to walk to a lot of the dancehalls with our high heels in a paper bag. We walked to the Crystal ballroom on a regular basis and at other times we went to Barry's Hotel and the National Ballroom. We also went to Kevin's Street Garda Station, which had dances on Sunday nights for 2 shillings and 6 pence, and to afternoon dances on Sundays in the Metropole Hotel. They were usually filled with medical students, Nigerian, Polish and Indian and one Nigerian took a fancy to me. He was a fantastic dancer and as I always loved dancing we danced the whole afternoon together. Then he said, 'I would love to take you back to Africa in a months time, as my dad said to bring back a white woman with me. Let`s go to a party tonight to get to know each other better. When I declined his offer he was furious but very persistent and at the time I thought it was hilarious.

We also travelled in a group and had such great fun, innocent fun. We had real joy in our hearts. If one laughed we all laughed and sometimes we did not even know what we were laughing at. Laughing is infectious, like the `flu. Nowadays I think people take life too seriously. Money is no problem for them, they work much shorter hours and they have better working conditions. One thing they lack is joy in their lives.

A lot of you would not remember the 'Teddy boy era' in Dublin. They went around in gangs and they had their own hairstyles, something like Elvis Presley`s. They covered their hair with Bryll cream and wore black suits with very narrow trousers and loose jackets with very broad shoulders. They wore black patent, pointed shoes. To me they looked like triangles. They looked very tough but really they were harmless. Once we had a patient in the hospital that was a member of the gang, his name was Brendan Dunne. He said with a smile, 'wait till I get out of here because if I ever meet you on the street I will embarrass you'. A week later he was discharged. I went for a walk up towards Harold's Cross and sure enough I ran into a group of 'Teddy boys'. They were sitting on a wall and it was late evening so the street was very quiet. I wore high-heeled shoes and the street being so quiet you could really hear the clickety click. The next thing was that the Teddy Boys started to sing, ' I had a good job and I left, I had a good job and I left', followed by 'Nursey Nursey, I am getting worsey'. I was very embarrassed, but at the same time I had to laugh as I thought it was so funny. Brendan Dunne was in the centre of the gang, enjoying every minute of it. I tried to keep a straight face, as I did not want to draw them on me, but, deep down, I too was enjoying the fun. Another day, on O' Connells bridge, I saw this old lady who had difficulty crossing the street as it was rush hour. Those teddy boys ran and helped her across the street, so you see they were like kiwi fruit, soft inside but with a rough appearance. You can not always judge a book by its cover.

I trained as a midwife in Scotland, in a small town 20 miles from Glasgow. I had the time of my life in Scotland and loved every minute of it. I had such kindness and love shown to me from everyone. I worked out on District and it was a wonderful experience for me.

Even in those days you had a lot of unmarried mothers and they were treated with scorn. One day I walked into this house where a 17-year-old girl was very near having her baby. Her name was Janet, she was a lovely friendly girl but unmarried, and she was very nervous and apprehensive. She had a very healthy pregnancy without any complications. I sat down beside her and told her there was nothing to be nervous about as women have babies every day and that I would stay with her until she had her baby. We were enjoying a lovely chat and she was beginning to relax when, all of a sudden, the door opened and in walked this big woman who was her mother. She stood over her with a sweeping brush and kept shouting at her, telling her she had brought disgrace on her family. I told her this was the wrong time to be angry with her daughter and spent a lot of time trying to calm this woman down and comfort the poor young girl. I was horrified that the mother was so angry when her daughter was screaming in pain. After a few hours she had a beautiful baby and when her mother saw it she softened.

On another day I visited a home of a very poor family. When I met Mary at the door she told me she was well on in labour and then she took me into the sitting room. When she said, 'I am now ready to make my bed', I understood her to mean clean linen but to my amazement this is what she did. She got some chairs and a mattress and used the settee for the head of her bed, and the chairs to support the mattress. Then she got a quilt and that was her bed made for delivery. I listened to the baby's heart and then I heard a peculiar noise coming from the corner and there was an alsation dog having pups. She never stopped till she had 10 of them and as Mary got more advanced in labour she gave the odd shout followed by a growl from Lassie in the corner. Then Lassie started to pass wind and I wanted to open the window, but froze because I was badly bitten by a dog when I was 11 years old and was hospitalised for 3 weeks.

Shortly after that Mary produced a bouncing baby girl and she called the baby after me as I stayed with her throughout her labour. Her little girl then walked in all dressed up in her dancing kilt which was decorated with medals she had won for dancing, followed by the rest of the family. I washed the baby and put it in its little cradle. The room under the stairs was off the sitting room and the little girl put Lassie and her brood in there - I was so glad to see the back of Lassie! Then the husband arrived with tea and I was afraid to drink the tea because of the dreadful smell in the room, but I said 'If it`s good enough for the people in this house it`s good enough for me'.

I worked in a poor area and I had a real love for the people. The work I did in Scotland has been of great help to me in the work I do now. I really got to know a lot of people and it was lovely and homely having their babies at home because they were always very relaxed with their families around them. If any complications should arise they could be in the hospital in 10 mins in the ambulance, as it was a small town. It was amazing how many families I got to know and how they all shared their problems with me and gave me wonderful presents to bring home when I left Scotland. They were very hospitable people and I always got tea and goodies in every house I visited.

One morning this lady rang at 7 a.m. saying she was Yvonne MacIntyre and to come quickly as she was having labour pains. Her house was in a very poor area of the town. When I arrived at the house the door was unlocked as they were expecting me and I walked into the bedroom to find Yvonne in bed with her husband and her 2-year-old baby. The smell from the room was horrible and her husband was still drunk after the night before. I caught the jeans on the back of a chair and gave them to him and then went outside the bedroom door while he put them on.

When I got back into the room the 2-year-old got out of the bed, threw her dirty nappy into the corner of the room and sat on her potty. When Yvonne shouted at her the child turned the potty over. Then she played with Yvonne's make up and she spilt the nail varnish on the bed. Somehow, in the middle of all this chaos I examined Yvonne and found she was well advanced in labour but, when I went to prepare the cot, to my amazement she had neither cot nor baby clothes. In those days you were given a grant from the health authority when you were 7 months pregnant to cover expenses and when I asked her 'what did you do with your grant money' she said they both drank it. When her little 10-year-old called to the door she was off to school and looked so smart in her school uniform. I told her to call to her next door neighbour for baby clothes and she arrived back with some in about 5 minutes. After about 2 hours Yvonne gave birth to a bouncing baby girl. 'Thank God it is all over' she said, 'this is my last wane'. When I asked her if she had decided on a name she said 'Och ay, I am going to call her Rennie as I lived on these bloody things throughout my pregnancy with all the heartburn I suffered'. Yvonne's mother arrived with hot water to bath the baby, and when I called in the father, who had sobered up at this stage, as well as the other children, they were all overjoyed to see the new baby. I then got one of the drawers from the chest of drawers and used   as a cot for the baby and finally we all had tea and cake. I visited Yvonne every day for a week to see how herself and Rennie were getting on. To my amazement she coped wonderfully. Her mother and the older children helped out and she gave me a lovely present for being kind to her when she was in labour.

Another time one of the doctors told me to call to see Margaret Campbell, as she had visited the clinic the day before and her blood pressure was high. Margaret lived in a lovely new house and when I visited it, I admired the way it was decorated. I took her blood pressure, which was very high and gave one look at her ankles, which were both swollen. Lastly I asked her for a specimen of urine, as I wanted to test it for protein. She had her 5 children around the table and she was giving all of them Cornflakes.

So she got a cup off the dresser and in 2 mins she was back with the sample of urine in the cup. I nearly died when I saw what she'd done. I tested it and sure enough there was protein in it. I hoped then that she would throw the cup in the bin, but I dared not ask because she became angry with one of the children when a jug of milk was turned over on the table. I advised her to go to hospital immediately but she insisted she wanted to have her baby at home. As luck would have it, though, she went into premature labour and was rushed to hospital at 8 months pregnant. Mother and baby survived. Pre-eclampsia in those days was very dangerous. That was one house I did not have tea in!

When I walked towards the corporation flats I would meet a crowd of kids and they knew at once who I was, as in those days we wore outdoor uniforms of navy coats and navy hats and we carried a suitcase with our equipment to deliver the babies. I had great fun with those kids, as they believed the baby was in the suitcase! Kids were so innocent in those days. Nowadays I think they grow up too quickly.

One bright sunny morning in mid June, Dr. James Wilson rang me to visit his house as his wife was in labour. It was a big house on the suburbs of the town. I approached it through a long avenue with beautiful chestnut trees on either side. As I drew nearer to it, I was amazed at the size of the house. It was their first baby and I said to myself what: "What on earth did they need all those rooms for." The house was painted white and the front door, a royal blue.

I met the doctor at the door and he seemed in a very bad mood. He said he was very annoyed with his wife as she refused to go to hospital to have her baby. I followed him upstairs into this very large room, with two big Georgian-type windows over-looking the lawn and the tennis court. He introduced me to his wife, Anne, who was well- advanced in labour. He told me he was after examining her so there was no need for me to examine her. She was a very nice lady. Then the doctor said:

"The obstetrician will be here shortly". He was the chief obstetrician for the West Coast of Scotland. The doctor was very nervous and he said: "I want you to deliver this baby and I want my wife to have no stitches and I also want no blood on my carpet, please". The carpet was white with red roses.

Shortly after, the obstetrician arrived. He was Dr. Peter McKay. He arrived in his wellington boots and a large overcoat. I knew he was a bit of a character. Then I said: "Hello" to him and he replied: "Hello Irish". He was a very jolly man of about sixty years and then he told about his love life and how he was divorced three times. He said he had just done some hillwalking. I was amused at his jokes and I knew instantly he was a very good doctor. He told me he was writing a book on the abnormalities in afterbirths. I knew he was a bit eccentric and I was delighted with his company as I thought the relationship with the doctor and his wife was strained.

After about an hour, Anne produced a lovely baby boy, and as luck would have it, and nothing to do with my skill, her baby was delivered without a stitch. I was not embarrassed in front of the doctors. I found delivering babies very easy work. She called her baby "Ian James". I then bathed the baby and the doctor invited me to stay for dinner. They had a lady in to do the cleaning and the cooking. I was looking forward to a nice meal, as I felt hungry after being in the house for a few urs.

Then Dr. Peter, Dr. Wilson and myself   dinner together. We got very little on our plates. You wouldn't give it to a snipe. Afterwards I got rice pudding made of water. Dr. Wilson watched every bite going into my mouth. I thought it's a true saying – "the bigger the house, the smaller the amount in the fridge." Then Dr. Peter and myself talked a lot, but mostly it was a case of listening to his love life. Dr. Wilson was bored because he was a bit of a snob and he was disgusted with Dr. Peter's "carry-on". When I looked across the table and saw Dr. Wilson's cross face, you would think " If he smiled his face would split." I really enjoyed Dr. Peter, as he was great fun. I said to myself this is better than the Theatre Royal with Jimmy O'Dea and Maureen Potter, our famous Irish comedians. I looked around the dining room at all the expensive antique furniture. This house was in sharp contrast to the houses I visited at the other end of town. As the saying goes: "One half do not know how the other half live."

I went upstairs to say goodbye to baby Ian James and his mother Anne. Dr. Peter said: "Do you have a boyfriend?". You're not a bad looking winch. If you wore lipstick and a smile, I think you might get a nice Scottish boyfriend." Then Dr. Peter and myself left together. I had heard of Dr. Peter before this --he was a very kind man to everyone. He was full of love. Dr. Peter had a beautiful bedside manner and he could relate to patients from every walk of life. The poor and the rich were all treated the same by him. If some of the patients were depressed, he would find something humerous to make them laugh, because as you know laughter is the greatest medicine for the depressed. (God is love and everyone that lives in love, lives in God – 1 John 4:16).

THE ONE WHO SAW ME CARED

In 1962 I met Brian and was really taken by his sense of humour and his gentleness. He was the apple of my eye and just being in his company made me feel special. I had longed so much to be loved, to be in the arms of someone special, because I never received love as a child. I wanted to be myself and not put on an act and I could take off my mask and be myself with Brian. He was the artist and I was the clay and, together, we moulded the way for each other. The more I got to know him the more I fell in love with him. It is a beautiful feeling to be loved and I was so lucky to meet Brian, as I would have fallen into any man's arms just to feel the warmth of someone's arms around me.

I really began to enjoy life as we cuddled, sang and danced together. We both loved dancing and that was the wonderful era of dance bands. We went to hear Michael O'Callaghan's band, The Bluebell quartet, The Ritz Show Band, the Cahalan brothers and many more. After a few months, Brian asked me to marry him and on the 13th of June 1963, the feast of Corpus Christi that year, we got engaged. I was so excited I was on cloud nine, showing off my 'sparklers' to everyone I met, and now that I was engaged I truly felt that I was special to someone.

Then my old enemy, the fears of my childhood, started to haunt me, because my Mother had told me all my life that I would never marry and no man would look at me. When I began to think about it I wondered if I would ever have children and whether my marriage would be a failure, or if the change in my lifestyle would be a success. Brian calmed all my fears. He had a soothing effect on me whenever I was upset and sometimes owing to my childhood I would over react to a minor thing. I think, myself, it is a fear of failure because if I made a wrong decision in childhood it gave Mother another excuse to beat me.

Mother and one of her friends caused me a lot of grief over my wedding. They decided how many guests I would have and whom each guest should be; they even went as far as telling the guests the presents I would like, but Mother still told me I would have to pay for everything. I had no say in anything, and you'd wonder who was getting married! Although I loved Brian to bits, I felt such stress that I was going to call off the wedding and emigrate to America, as America was crying out for Irish nurses in the 1950s and 1960s. I even went as far as the travel agency and then I thought it would not be fair to Brian. Mother and her ally tried to control my life so completely that I felt I was a 3-year-old child again. They both had the same personality and Mother's feelings, together with the jealousy of the other, because I was the younger and getting married before her, meant they made life hell for me. I had holiday due to me coming up to my wedding day, but decided to work and just take a week off before the wedding, as I could not cope with the abuse I was getting. I never got on with this girl, as we are so very different, and all my life when she saw Mother being nasty, she joined in. As she had her own cruel little tactics to bring me down, and by God they worked! I was timid and always obedient because I was afraid, and as a result I was always treated as if I were inferior, and made an outcast. My relationship with mother's friend, has not changed much over the years, but we have grown to tolerate each other. She doesn't affect me any more in the way she did and I no longer feel trapped. She told so many lies about me, making me out to be someone I never was, and I do not know why she tried to turn Mother even more against me. I always knew what she'd done, because it all came back to me the next time I met Mother. I forgive her for what she has done because she too was hurt in life.

We got married on the 7th of Oct. 1963, on the feast of Our Lady of the Holy Rosary, as I had a great devotion to the rosary after I had an awesome experience with Our Lady when I was 12 years old. When I married Brian I thought I was stepping into Heaven, and there was no going back. I felt so proud walking down the aisle with this handsome man, who was six foot four inches tall. I always loved tall men. We toured all over Northern Ireland on our honeymoon. When we arrived in Omagh we knew nothing about roundabouts as we had nothing like them down in the South so we parked in the wrong place and a lovely little policeman told us to move on. As soon as he was out of sight, though, we left the car where it was and went shopping. Unfortunately, when we went back, we met the same policeman and this time he was very angry with us and sent us to the police station with some tickets for breaking the law. At the station, when the sergeant asked us our business in Omagh and we told him we were on our honeymoon, he laughed, tore up the tickets and told us to get out of Omagh before we were given any more. I thought this was a very nice gesture and I never forgot it.

In my marriage with Brian, it was all give and take and we had to learn from each other. Deep down I think Brian was a lonely man as he found it hard to mix with people. We lived on an isolated farm and I found the country life lonely and depressing. I felt chained to a way of life that did not suit my personality; it was like being back home again as a child with the lonely fields and the strain of living without people around me. Because of my eyesight I never drove, and this made life more difficult, as I was completely dependent on Brian to go anywhere I needed to go. Brian was my Heaven but the farm was my hell and I would have given any money to be set free from that loneliness. When I got up in the morning I had nobody to talk to once Brian was out working on the farm. Brian inherited this farm from his father and he felt obliged to carry on working it. I asked him to leave it but he felt that if he left the farm his life would be empty, as all he knew was farming. His father lived with us and he was a very nice old man, who hated farming and only barely had enough money to get by. He loved gardening and should have really gone into horticulture, and was an avid reader and a wonderful conversationalist. We had a lot in common and he helped me with the garden. I loved his company and we had only been married seven months when he had a severe stroke and went to God in a few weeks. I missed him so much because he was like a second father to me.

In our life together, Brian and I had a lot of ups and downs and a lot of smiles and frowns together. We tolerated the burdens and tried to see the fun in them. God blessed us with 5 children, 2 boys and 3 girls and Brian loved his children dearly, especially when they were small, as he was very good with young ones. My husband was a very loving man all through our marriage, but he could never talk about his childhood, which made him sink into despair at times. He was a very private person and a loyal friend and a loyal husband to me. We encountered great times together. It broke my heart when he became ill, and in later life the man I loved changed so much, but I still had to accept the chance and do the best I could for the sake of my children.

I suffered from ill health a lot of my life, and I was very close to death many times, even as a child. Jesus told me on one occasion that my life could have gone either way. I often neglected my body and this was a big mistake. I worked very, very hard and I got burnt out on many occasions but I had to work so hard because Brian became ill and I needed to make the money to rear my children. I did not realise that neglecting your body was a sin and that God wants us to see after our bodies as well as our souls. Our bodies are the temples of the Holy Spirit. Today, I have to take a rest in case I slip back into old habits. Brian died in 1996 so we had 33 good years and happy times together. We had an exquisitely happy life together and I praise God for the good he showed to us.

' If we are living now by the Holy Spirit, Let us follow the Holy Spirit leading in every part of our lives' Gal 25

A LOVE THAT IS SO PROFOUND

My love for you is like the sea; it has no width,
No beginning and no end, for you it fits,
It flows from river to ocean and from there to the sea,
And I am sure yours is the same foe me.
Over rocks it may flow and at times be slow
But my love for you is always go,
And need never be uprooted because it was only once sown.
It has no shape, as do the stones
If you knew ,my love it is so profound
That it has no distractions and no bounds.
I could only love you and no one else,
And in my heart my love for you melts,
to be near your side and to be in your arms,
In life it has made me so calm.
Things between us will never change ,
Even sometimes when they seem out of range ,
My love for you will be the same forever more,
Because the bottom line is, you and Jesus are my core

DEDICATED TO BRIAN

My loving husband, what joy you gave to me in life.
You gave me the strength to strive,
We had our ups and downs to go through
But God gave us His loving cure.
Hand in hand we were led
You were my joy, you were everything
That a heavenly father on earth could bring.
God is the great wonderful king
He gave me you so I was sheltered under your wing.
A pouring joined together as one,
Without Our Lady it would never have being done,
This grace was born in us and it is eternal,
This fill was the Lord's own will,
The greatest force , we are in God's shadow,
This power goes everywhere with us ,even through the meadow,
This lasting peace knowing we are a bonding grace,
Puts delight in the Lord for his grace we have tasted.

FROM THE PAIN TO THE JOY

When my 3rd child was born I noticed a cataract on her right eye and when she was ten months old I took her to an eye specialist. He advised me to put her in hospital right away for surgery, as the sight in her other eye was not perfect. He said she would not miss me at this age as parents were not allowed to stay overnight in the hospital at that time. I also had her examined by a paediatrician. I rang the doctor after the operation and he told me that the operation was unsuccessful, as there was calcium in the cataract. Then he performed another operation and this operation was not a success either. When I went to collect her from hospital after two weeks the nun in charge of the ward told me she was in great health and had put on weight.

As soon as I took her home I realised that there was something wrong. My baby could not sit, or hold her head up, and when I put her sitting up she just fell down like a lump of jelly. I noticed all her muscles were atonic. She cried with a high pitched cry and had no eye contact with me. A neighbour came to visit me and said, ' it would have been better to bring her home dead rather than half dead'. I began to feed her on milk like a week old baby as she could not swallow solid food and when I contacted the paediatrician he was very rude to me and gave me no explanation. The eye specialist said, that she was the same going into hospital but that I had not noticed. I was so hurt and humiliated by the way the doctors treated me. All I wanted was the truth about the mistakes made and I had no intention of going to law. I thought my little girl had no future and my heart was broken in two. I felt as if my little baby had been taken away and I found I had not the strength to cope. I could only place my hope in God, the greatest King and Lord.

I thought I would get pity from my Mother, but she said 'I should not have listened to the doctors and that nothing could be done about it now'. She asked why I could not have waited until she was five or six years old and what had been the hurry in sending her for surgery. When I told Brian what my mother had said, he said perhaps we should have waited for a little while. Then my older sister came and said likewise. Jesus said, ' judge not and you will not be judged'. I judged myself and became full of self-hatred guilt and bitterness because I felt I had murdered my own child. I hated myself so much that I felt, if a bus went over me on the road it would be doing an act of kindness for society. I felt God could not love me either, but God never let go of my hand during this time.

God put a nice doctor in my way who listened to me and stood by me, and we became great friends during those difficult years. Fiona became more difficult, and I now had 2 other babies to care for. A doctor from Scotland came on holiday to my guesthouse and he diagnosed Fiona as being autistic, and said that the operation for cataracts was performed in Scotland on babies from six months upwards. It was like winning the Lotto because he was the only man who gave me hope.

When Fiona was three years old I could no longer care for her, so I sent her to a hospital for children for special needs. I missed my little girl, and I was always wondering if she was happy and well cared for, in this hospital run by nuns. To my horror, she was abused in the hospital. I was aware of the beatings from an early stage, as she was able to tell me. She arrived home one day with a mark on her back and told me that she had been beaten. I asked her why she was beaten and she told me that a young girl was in charge of them at night and she told her if she went to the toilet at night she would be beaten, and if she wet the bed she would also be beaten. She sneaked out to the toilet when everything was quiet but she was caught going back to bed and got a savage beating. I asked my Mother for advice, as I was too broken to make a decision on my own, but she just said to do nothing as I was very lucky that the nuns had taken my child in. Fiona is very short sighted but she was made to sit on a stool at the back of the room to watch the T.V. She could not see it and every time she got off the stool she was beaten. She also went to a school for people with special needs and was also beaten there. As she was autistic she could not understand so she sat on the floor and pulled all her hair out. When she told me her horror stories, hearing her little cries was like a knife piecing my heart.

Fiona was battered on the head with bare fists and this nun called herself a Sister of Charity. Where was the Christian charity in this treatment of defenceless little children? These nuns did this work in the name of Jesus but took their anger out on little children. They had their pets and for the rest they didn't care.

She was beaten with hairbrushes, and any thing they could get hold of. The nun in charge of the ward told the workers to beat her. The general public thought the nuns were doing wonderful work for those children but were unaware of the cruelty that went on behind closed doors. They were dressed very well and had their hair done up in ringlets when they were going home for a holiday.

It broke my heart, and I suffered so much guilt, shame and remorse when I did nothing about it, because I was too broken. She used to come home on holiday and she did not like going back. Parting with her was nothing compared to the guilt I suffered from putting her into a hospital where she was unhappy. They dressed her up beautifully for coming home and did her hair with great style but the cruelty behind the scenes was covered up.

She is not fully healed yet of the entire emotional trauma she suffered there. Shortly before she left, she informed the nun in charge about the abuse and it stopped immediately, but the person who abused her still stayed on in employment. The nun in charge of the ward knew what was happening but did nothing about it.

I had a very good friend and on one occasion, when I was upset at parting with Fiona, she said, 'never mind Eileen, the nuns will look after her with love'. Her words still ring in my ears as I am only now being healed of that period in my life. It took a long time to forgive the nuns and to forgive myself. I cried for other children, the poor little retarded children who were not able to tell their parents. But then I said to myself, what pain it saved them.

I then started to pray to Little Nellie of Holy God, for Fiona, because Little Nellie, an Irish child saint who suffered so much as a child. God answered my prayer in a miraculous and wonderful way. She was now 8 years old, I had a phone call from the hospital, saying that Fiona had made a miraculous recovery and that she was now ready to go home. It was arranged when she entered the hospital that they would keep her until she was sixteen years I was so happy when I went to collect her, because I could see at once that Fiona was cured of autism. She ran towards me and gave me a big hug and said mammy I love you. Little Nellie not only cured Fiona but she also cured me from guilt and I could now forgive the doctors, the nuns and all those who ill treated Fiona. When she came home she went to the local national school. Where she met a very kind teacher who took great interest in her. Then she went on to Secondary school, and did her Leaving Cert. Fiona is now a young woman living an independent life. She worked as a care assistant in a hospital for four years and is now working with the elderly. God has turned her pain into joy. She now has a powerful gift of prayer. God has now healed me of self-hatred, layer by layer.

Blessed are those who trust in the Lord and have made the Lord their hope and confidence' Ger. 17

' WHAT YOU DO TO THE LEAST OF MY BROTHERS YOU DO IT TO ME'

I praise the Lord for what he has achieved for her. The emotional scars are gradually being healed in God's love and mercy. For all you little children, who have suffered in the same way in the hands of carers, come forward today and tell your story of what happened to you. It will be the first day of your healing, it will help you to come closer to God and God will give you the grace to forgive. Many years of your life may have been stolen but don't let them take any more. Let this day be the first day of the rest of your life. The truth will set you free. Jesus came on earth to set the captives free because Jesus is the way, the truth, and the life.

FIONA'S OWN STORY

The prison cell for the child that was unwell.
When I was a child I suffered pain,
It was so severe it came down like the rain,
Being kept from my mother,
And also my sisters and brothers.
At the hands of others I did suffer,
These people were stronger than me and tougher.
They pulled my hair they did not care
They just looked in my eyes their glancing stare.
My body and my clothes they did tear,
Two of them together they made a mighty pair.
They beat me and slapped me and then they would flee,
They laughed and made fun
That was their work done
Visiting my mother when I could
at least we were together
My mothers heart and my heart together were joined.
She was my only joy
It was like a gift on high.
Returning to those sisters
I was afraid I might get more blisters,
I hoped in the Lord all would change,
That I would no longer have marks or physical pains.
The physical marks may go
My mental scars were a blow,
The day I heard I was going home ,
I wanted to write a poem.
My life was sorrow and it turned to joy,
Because I knew when I met mammy my old life was gone by
When they beat me I always asked the question why?
At times I felt I would rather die
My life has moved on with my mom
And I have a great bond

Of me she is so fond,
She is so gentle and so calm ,
She would never allow me any harm.
I have grown up now,
And to God I should bow
Only for my mothers prayers
The one in my life who most cares.
I have been healed layer by layer,
Jesus has been more than fair
Because in His ocean of mercy,
I never again will be thirsty
I have achieved what most people have.
And at the end of it all I still can laugh
Without my mother I would have been lost .
But she too paid the cost .
My mother suffered in my losses and gains
In my tears and in my pains
I will forgive and forget,
Because in my life a great God I have met
I praise His name
Because into my life He came,
I give Him glory,
Because He has healed me of my life
And this is my story.

Chaplet to Little Nellie

O Little Nellie, protect your little ones through the power of our Lord Jesus Christ, from being crucified. Save their suffering O little one. Say 9 times.

Amen.

A Prayer of Healing for Those that were Abused

Lord Jesus, heal the wounds of my soul, the wounds that are so deep and are full of holes. Fill my wounds up with your most precious blood, so that the wounds will be no more. Help me to forgive and forget memory lane. Bring me up the lane of the future with you, Lord, so I can live my life to the full.

Amen

Jesus the Divine Physician

Come Lord Jesus, and fill my temple with your Glory and your light. Wash over my scars, Lord, which have been so deep and that wounded me because of my past. Shed your blood on my wounds and heal me according to your will.

Help me, Lord, to forgive myself for hating myself all those years. Help me to forgive the doctors and the nuns for not showing me understanding, and for not telling me the full truth.

Help me, Lord, to forgive other members of society who did not fill their role in helping me during my suffering.

Heal all these people, Lord, who hurt me knowingly or unknowingly and do something nice for these people today. In your name I ask you to give them a new outpouring of the Holy Spirit and lead them into your heavenly light and guidance.

Amen

THE LIFE OF LITTLE NELLIE

When I was five years old, after I had an eye operation, my mother took me up to Sunday's Well in Cork City to visit Little Nellie's grave. I also went to see her little bedroom and was completely overwhelmed by my visit. There was a little spiral staircase leading to her room and everything was just as it had been when she was living there. I even saw her little iron bed and personal belongings. Her grave itself is in the nuns' cemetery and has a statue of the Infant of Prague on her headstone, as she was so devoted to the Infant Jesus, calling him her Holy God. Little Nellie was known all over Cork as Little Nellie of Holy God, the violet of the Holy Eucharist.

Fiona's childhood and Little Nellie's were very similar as they were both abused by people who looked after them. I am greatly devoted to her as she worked a miracle in my daughter, Fiona's life when she was a child.

Little Nellie had her own statue of the Infant of Prague in her bedroom. One day she took her trumpet out from among her toys, stood the statue on the floor and blew the trumpet, saying 'now Little Jesus, dance for me'. When she got tired and could no longer play she told her nurse (Nurse Hall), that Jesus danced to her music and when she stopped playing, He stopped dancing.

Little Nellie was born in Waterford on 24th August 1903. Her family moved to Spike Island in Cork Harbour in 1905 and she had two brothers and one sister. Nellie's mother, Mary, suffered from consumption, which was very prevalent in Ireland at the turn of the century. As Little Nellie was Mary's youngest sister she loved her dearly and taught her to kiss the crucifix, a habit she always retained.

Mary Organ died in 1907 and asked Jesus, before she died, to look after her baby. Little Nellie and her sister were put in an orphanage in The Good Shepherd Convent in Cork City and her brothers were sent to one in Upton, County Cork, that was managed by the Christian Brothers.

Nellie was thin and frail and a delicate little girl. She complained to the Nuns of a sore throat and backache and when the doctor examined her back he discovered that she had a curve in her spine. When he looked in her throat he discovered, to his amazement, that a tooth had grown there and after he had extracted it Little Nellie looked up at the nun and said, " Mother, do you believe me now, that my throat was sore?" The nuns were harsh in those days.

She was a lonely little girl and played on her own, her days full of tears and pain. All she received was cruelty; slaves were treated better than she was and her life was made hell by the people who cared for her. She was a child in a prison cell, afraid of her own shadow, with no one to turn to and no way out. The nuns had their pets and she was not one of them. They used her as a way of getting rid of their own anger. There were children there who were treated well but she was left to fight for herself and cried herself to sleep so often that she complained of pain in her face from crying.

Then she turned to God because she had nowhere else to turn and spent all her short life praying. God listened to her and gave her such comfort that she realised He could help her. However, the nuns became jealous of her because she received such wisdom and they could see God shining through her. The nuns at that time were proud. People thought they were wonderful to take in orphans and looked up to them as gods but they did not treat Nellie well and she taught them everything they needed to know about prayer.

Nuns were not saints in those days because many were unhappy and were not suited to that way of life. They were unkind to the children because of their own bitterness. They never thought that a child could have gifts. Nellie suffered a lot at their hands and was like a prisoner of war fighting her own battles. Every year of her life was a struggle and happiness never existed for her after she left home.

Peoples` lives are ruined today over evil acts that affected their childhood and we need to break the chain of suffering for little children. We need to let people know what they do wrong, no matter who they are, even if they are priests or nuns.

The one thing that kept Nellie going was that she had a great gift of acceptance. Consumption was destroying the frame of her little body; not only were her lungs wasting away but her jaw, too, began to crumble. She never complained but just grasped her crucifix.

Developing a great love for the Eucharist, she would say, when exposition was on, "take me to the chapel, I know Holy God is not in the lock-up today." Nellie told the nuns that she had a longing to receive Holy Communion and received special permission from the Bishop. This was most unusual as in those days children did not take the Eucharist until they were ten years old and she was only four. After she received Holy Communion she went into ecstasy, she was in a world of her own with her Holy God.

Dr.O'Callaghan, who was then the Bishop of Cork, administered the sacrament of confirmation in 1907 as she was very weak and the nuns thought her near death. She understood all about the gifts of the Holy Spirit and the sacrament of Confirmation and declared to all, "I am now a soldier of Holy God", showing heroic strength and patience in her suffering.

She was able to tell the nuns if they did something wrong such as missing Mass. One day she was asked to pray for a request to be answered and was able to say that Holy God knew and that was enough. When she looked out of the window from her little bed she called the clouds the friends and angels of God. After she received communion she might be in ecstasy for hours.

Little Nellie flew to God on 2ndFebruary 1908 and was buried in St.Joseph's cemetery. Soon afterwards one of the nuns had a dream that Nellie wished to have her remains removed to the convent cemetery. Permission was granted and when the grave was opened a year and a half later her body was found to be intact; her hands were flexible and her nails and hair had grown. The Holy Communion dress and veil that she had been buried in were also perfect and the silver medal and blue ribbon

THE TEARS I CRIED, HE DRIED

of the sodality of Our Lady was so bright that it looked as if it had been newly polished.

The Pope requested a relic from Bishop O`Callaghan after her death. Little Nellie has worked a lot of miracles in peoples` lives, especially for children as in my daughter, Fiona's, case.

Little Nellie has a special place in my holy garden and one chapel is dedicated to her in her honour.

LITTLE NELLIE PRINCESS OF JESUS

Little princess, pure white star,
In Jesus' love you are near, not far,
Through humble little words, spoken by a child
Jesus' mantle of prosperity did you enfold.
Your words showed the wisdom and knowledge of truth,
When adults heard you they would pause, stand mute,
Your precious life was a journey to teach adults,
The love of Jesus ,and convert their faults,
You were a child in years and adult in wisdom,
God chose you ,that's how He did come.
To pass on His message, through you to this nation.
He chose you to teach His creation to be patient,
You would help them give their troubled minds to Him in surrender,
You knew so young that Jesus was your defender,
And when you were in pain He gave you ease,
You were happy that Jesus love would never cease,
His love increased day by day more and more,
Until you felt no longer sore,
Grant us little Nellie blessings to know God better,
In our soil to trust Him to be the setter.

LITTLE NELLIE'S BREASTPLATE

O little Nellie chosen child of God who did as the Lord asked spoke His words of truth. You helped those in need who needed God's scripture to feed on. Your suffering was severe and you did not forsake Him during your trials. Your life was empty but you gave it a meaning you were filled with the gifts of the holy spirit

People have been healed ,because of your prayers . You endured great suffering, but you knew God would reward you. Your life is a testimony for everyone, to hear how you developed in the maturity of spirit , which was a way beyond your years.

We pray through your intercession to help all little children who are suffering .O Little Nellie protect the lives of little children who are suffering. Through your intercession we make our prayers known to God.

WHEN LITTLE NELLIE'S STOCKING WENT MISSING

As the years flow by other stories unfold. I am running and racing, trying to please the hundreds coming through my gate; praying and reasoning with every kind of suffering, from marriage problems to serious illnesses to minor issues. They all come to receive the gift of God.

The stories that I listen to in one day alone would fill a book about the problems people have in life. It can be so hard because I take everyone in their turn to pray with and counsel. Some people arrive with very sick children and, if they are kept waiting, they can get very impatient. I encourage them to be at peace with themselves and others. As I pray with them I ask for God's calmness to come upon them, so that they may be still and know their Master. It is only when they are tranquil that God gives His power of healing to meet each one's need. I make people realise that I am only a tool and nothing more than that. He is the all-powerful God. I give them words of encouragement and the words of scripture that come to my mind for each individual. I believe that God does, indeed, work in very mysterious ways, especially for the people who come to my garden.

I have a little pouch and in it I hold the relics of saints. I have first class relics such as those of St.Vincent Palloti, St.Vincent De Paul and Little Nellie (a Cork saint) and second class relics of various saints. There are different classes of relics; first class are items such as bone or hair, second class are clothing and third class something that has touched either first or second. Many people today have relics that are third class.

Such items are powerful because they are proof that God touched those people in a very special way when they were alive and that they devoted their whole lives to doing God's works of mercy. They lived in self-denial and made every sacrifice for their God, no matter what the situation or circumstance. When they died they were recognised as especially holy people and were first beatified and then canonised as saints, but only after miracles had been performed through their intercession.

When miracles happen through their prayers before the throne of God, powerful healing takes place and then people look for a relic. That in itself can cure. A relic of a saint is a symbol of God's power, because what He has done in a saint's life He can do in ours; rocks can be moved from our paths and we can find peace.

Holding relics give me new hope but also brings to my mind the need to confess my sins. I open my heart and become more positive and realise that without Him I am nothing, empty, only the dust of the earth. I am like the salt that has gone tasteless. It was only by chance that I received them and I am a person who believes that grace should be shared. For the last three years I have kept them all in one pouch and when I pray with anyone, I know that God is using me as His instrument.

About two years ago a lady walked through my gate with a stocking from Little Nellie and this is a relic I really love because it was through her intervention that my daughter was healed. I feel that her stocking is a part of my life. I, too, was taken out of despair and given hope with her help. I had the opportunity of living life to the full again.

About Christmas 2004 a large group of people entered my garden and I prayed with each one individually. They all went away happy. Later on that night a lady rang me for prayer as she was in great turmoil but, to my horror, when I went to look for my pouch it was gone. I never blamed anyone else because I do have a habit of losing things at times. But I was terribly disappointed and upset and felt that the greatest treasure had gone from my home; a dark cloud had come over me. I asked everyone I knew to pray for me and I appealed especially to St.Anthony, as he is the patron saint of lost items. Three weeks later there was still no sign of it. Then, on Tuesday 1st February, I received a letter. To my horror a woman wrote to explain in great detail how her cousin had taken it when she was here and then passed it on to her. She, herself, decided to send it to all her family members, here and in England, so that they would get a blessing and a healing. I have given my testimony both here and in England so the people who have heard me know that Little Nellie is a powerful saint. Apparently, among other incidences of healing, someone was cured of Hodgkin's disease.

However, when it was posted back to this lady it was lost in the post, and, as everyone knows when something is lost in the post, 90% of the time it never turns up again. This is what worried me so much because I thought I'd never see it again. I was furious that someone would betray me like this. I had welcomed that family into my home, with open arms, and helped them because I trust people, no matter what class they come from.

She said that she wrote out of guilt that her family had cheated me and she wanted to own up. She knew that if she did not write, then no one else would, and apologised again and again while praying that it would be returned. She had tried to come to my house but had been afraid to face me, knowing that I would have said very little to her. I started to doubt God because I had been doing God's work when it happened. I suppose everyone has setbacks when they are working for God. It is as if the devil is trying to stop you, and I was angry and hurt, but I still continued on. I placed my trust in God that the stocking would be returned.

For years and years I had tried to get a relic of Little Nellie and had even asked the priests to help me, but they too were refused. Getting Nellie's stocking in the first place had been a miracle, as if I had truly 'found a treasure in a field, that no one else could steal', and I knew that if it should be returned it would be another miracle.

I think I knew in my heart that it would only be gone for a short while because I believed from the beginning that the stocking was for me so that I could share its grace with others. Then on Monday 7th February I heard that it had returned but even as I thanked God I read down through the letter and my happiness turned to sadness. I felt so angry that I wanted to give up all that I was doing for God. Despite what had happened the lady planned to send it off again to a friend who was ill and other friends wanted to cut it up so that they could each have a piece. She claimed it could not bother me because I had the other stocking, but, of course, I only ever had one. After telling me how sorry she was she showed me she did not care at all. As I continued to read I realised how upset I really was about the whole occurrence. It was a fright to think that I had helped these people and that is how I was repaid.

The woman also said that her cousin was cursing my garden because she could not understand how God heals some and not others. By cursing it she thought that she could put a stop to any healing visitors might receive. Obviously, this woman is very bitter with life and thinks it unfair for others to be healed and happy but God is stronger than any evil and I pray that she will be converted and drop the devil's tactics.

So I surrendered the situation to God and asked that His will be done, not mine and that I would try to be patient and understanding. At the same time I could have done without such stress at this hour of my life. I prayed also that He would guide the mind of the lady who had written the letters, and that He would give her the insight to realise that I needed the stocking as part of my ministry.

As time passed I received another two letters with the same garbage about how the stocking was travelling on a day to day basis but had come to terms by this time with what had happened. God can turn around any situation. Healing had been done, after all, so it was as if Little Nellie was walking around performing her own little miracles.

I waited patiently every day for the stocking to be returned and then on Friday 18th February it came in the post, just the same as the day it was stolen. If the lady had never written to me I would never have known the whereabouts of the relic. Knowing I had not lost it put my mind at ease and it was as if God was telling me what was happening to it. But it also made me angry and the content of those letters was very hurtful - it was as if the devil was eating away at me.

As I can see now this was another wonderful miracle performed by trusting in God. I forgive this lady and her cousins for what they put me through and am very grateful and thankful to God for a happy ending to this story.

THE GUESTHOUSE

Then the loneliness of the farm got to me. Loneliness could drive you to despair. I was always a deep thinker so I knew I needed a new outlet and I decided I was going to do something about it. I had three options; one was to go back to nursing as I missed hospital life so much with all my friends and all the craic. I knew this was not possible as I had two babies and I was expecting a third and I was too far away from any hospital with no form of transport. The second option was to sell the farm and move on. I knew Brian loved me but he felt that if he left the farm he would feel empty. He knew of no other way of life except farming and loved the animals and all that went with them. The third option was to open my house as a guesthouse. Brian was very much against this idea at first, as he was an extremely private person. He did not like the idea of strangers going through his home, so I made an entrance from the farmyard to the back of the house.

We opened our home as a farm guesthouse in 1967. It was the best move I ever made. We had no money and lived in a big old house that needed a lot of repair but had nine bedrooms that were large and airy. However, it was also cold and damp and I had to borrow money to modernise it. I loved the guesthouse although I knew very little about cooking, but practice makes perfect and some of the guests gave me recipes as well! I had wonderful people staying with me who were more like family than guests after a while. The same people came year after year and some of them are still my best friends. One family came every year for 17 years.

I ran the guesthouse for a long, hard, 22years and a lot of the time it was a struggle. I worked very hard, up to 14 or even 16 hours a day. My children served at the table from a very young age and always supported me and did as I asked. I knew it was hard on them, as it was their school holidays but I also knew that they enjoyed it, as they had the company of the

guests' children. I paid them well and also had other girls helping me. My children enjoyed playing with other children and it
helped them develop socially. They were fascinated with all the
different accents from other countries. My son once said to a
Scottish boy, 'You do not speak properly', and the child's father
thought it was hilarious. Regardless of what adults feel, when
children makes friends it's forever and separating them can be
traumatic. They do not think like adults. It was hard on my
children too but they were always excited about the new visitors. My children thought they were in the playground every
day as they had so many kids around and the others were fascinated at the way my own worked and served at table. Then after
a short while they offered to help too, as they wanted praise
from their parents. As the saying goes 'every cloud has a silver
lining' and for my children the guest's children were the linings.
They played on the swings and the slide and as kids go they
had very few rows. The parents played football. Everyone got
involved in the playground after his evening dinner. The young
ones used to make me very happy and I had parties for their
birthdays and special occasions.

What made my job very interesting was meeting people from
other countries and learning about all their different cultures.
Much of what I heard opened my eyes. It was wonderful being
in the company of pleasant people, as most people are happy on
holiday. It seemed that one minute I was terribly isolated and
lonely and now I had so many people around me that I could not
cope. My life was like a Christmas tree. I had to wait for every
light to go out, one by one, before I went to bed. That's how
busy I was but I enjoyed every minute of it. I had light in my life
and a sense of happiness and when people are happy they give
themselves more goals and they aim for them. My work started
at 7 O' clock every morning and I served breakfast at 9.00a.m.
to up to thirty people, including babies and children. Then each
family got a packed lunch when they were going out for the day.
Evening dinner was served at 6 p.m., tea and home baking at 10
p.m. and I did babysitting after that sometimes up to 2 a.m.

Then I decided to get mobile homes, as I could not accommodate all the people that wanted to stay in my guesthouse. I
started small as if planting a small shrub and over the years it
grew into a tree. My tree had many branches. The branches
were the people I came to know and they became great friends
of mine. They are still my friends but unfortunately some have
passed away over the years. We used to socialise together and
I organised a party every Friday night for my guests as a lovely
finale to their holiday.

My schedule in the guesthouse was crazy. My first priority
was each and every one of the guests and I never listened to my
own body calling. The minute lightning flashed I dashed to get
my work done. I never took any short cuts, other wise the tree
would have fallen down on me and the business would have
failed. Sometimes I felt frustrated with the children and the
guests and with so much work needing to be done. I used to say
to God ' I want to feel your presence and do your work ` and I
felt that I was doing God's work. The guests were my congrega-
tion. You would think that so much going on at home would
have affected Brian's and my own relationship, but I thank God
that this never happened. It actually brought us closer together.
Brian always loved small children and the guests` children used
to love being out in the farmyard with him, watching him milking the cows and feeding the animals.

None of my family was ever deprived and they were always happy. We were lovingly tied and united to each other.
Although I never received love as a child, I was always able to
give great love and affection to my children and was always
giving them hugs and kisses and telling them that I loved them.
We would often have an old sing song at night with the guests
getting involved as well. No one cared about making fools of
themselves and it was so relaxing. We were definitely all one
big happy family.

Because there were so many different cultures we had all
different kinds of songs but no matter what it was we all felt at
ease. Sometimes I would stop and say to myself 'Lord you have
given me a voice, make me use my voice to worship You'.

In the room there was no conductor or audience to please and no coloured lights, just songs we sang to one another. I often had people from Dublin who worked in the entertainment business and with the Dublin wit I could listen to them all night. So you see the guests put 'an upbeat' in my life. One minute I had an empty old house and now it was full to the brim. What I had been wanting in my whole life I now had. I pined for people and to feel at ease with them and the visitors used to tell me stories that would make me laugh. At the end of the day nothing beats the satisfaction of an honest day's work and making people happy. Everything I did in the guesthouse was self-taught, apart from the visitors giving me advice from time to time. The best teaching is our own mistakes.

I grew stronger by the day with the help of the Lord and I knew one day I would never worry about what people thought of me. So you see that's what my visitors did for me; I believe in myself, and nowadays it would take a lot to bring me down.

I was around people who paid me compliments and it was like being on a cloud with angels. They were so obliging that they would do anything that I asked of them. Since I never drove they would often take me up to the shop.

After I married Brian my luck changed. The hard-boiled world I had once known had softened and my solitary life was over. Even other people noticed the difference, as I became more assertive. When I looked at the clear blue sky I realised that there was no blindness in my eyes any more. The sky seemed to reflect my gaze. It was as if someone had taken a pair of scissors and cut me free. Although I had worked 14 hours a day I was very fresh. I was now among people where compassion existed and what a lovely feeling it was. I had won the marathon but although I knew now that I was successful in life, when I thought of my mother it was like an alarm sounding or the buzzing of an angry bee in my ear. I still loved setting tough goals for myself and I wanted people to be proud of me.

I set goals for my spiritual life but at this stage I was more successful in business. I hoped God would be patient with me but I knew there was plenty of time to grow spiritually. When I

awoke in the morning God was my adrenaline and it was working well. I used to look forward to the day even though at times
my head would ache and go crazy with all the people wanting
different things. I kept saying 'push yourself and the headaches
will go away` but I was pushing myself too much and I did not
realise that it was a sin to neglect your body. Even today I have
to watch myself in case I slip back into old habits. Our bodies
are the temples of the Holy Spirit. I did not care or worry about
my health. I laughed so much and felt that that was my best
medicine. I did not think that over stretching myself was a danger to my health. I knew my family was already proud of me
and I said to myself that I must slow down because life is not a
race but a journey. That's what the guesthouse taught me. Life
is a journey with God where you can be guided, or a journey
into the unknown world of disaster. I took the road to God.

One evening I went to collect eggs from a neighbour who
used to keep a lot of hens. I gathered together all the children
and my own kids as well. There were sixteen of us in all. Off I
went across the fields with my basket. We all sang and danced
across the field and I thought it was so beautiful to be in their
company. On my return I met two very concerned parents.
They were German and as they never let their children out of
their sight, they had become very worried. Even though they
were a little annoyed at first, when they heard them singing
with the rest of the children they were amazed. Germans are
inclined to be very strict with their children. They are wonderful people to have as guests and I always found them straight
forward and honest. I have been invited to Germany many
times and also to different parts of England. With the children
and the work on the farm we never managed to go anywhere
apart from a week in England with the Reeves family. English
people are very easy going and their children are always well
mannered. In August 1980, one English lady who was last in at
night, tried to take the key out of the door but failed. She approached me the following morning looking very anxious and
told me the tale about the door. When I told her it had been
stuck in the door for fifteen years she found it hard to believe.

Nowadays you would not leave your key in the door for one day let alone fifteen years.

My guesthouse was a circle of friends and the local people loved having them around as it brought business to the pubs and shops in the area. The local people loved chatting to the guests, as life was very quiet in the country and it gave them an interest and broadened their outlook on life. The nicest parts of my guesthouse were the mobile homes as they were so private. They had their own television, toilet facilities and fitted kitchen so the guests could make tea at any time they wished. That's one of the reasons why they were always booked out from year to year. West Cork is very scenic and it is full of unspoilt beaches, which makes it a great tourist attraction. The guesthouse was only fifteen minutes drive from the nearest sandy beach.

'Thank you' was a word that was always used when my guests were leaving and it was so nice to feel appreciated. It made my inside and outside smile. 'Thank you' did not exist in my childhood. I love meeting people and it gave me great confidence. It made all the bad words that were said to me wash away. It gave me a sense of self-worth even on days when I did not feel like working because I was so tired. Their very company made me so happy to do what I was doing. I had a visitor's book for my guests so I would remember each guest by name and some of them wrote very encouraging comments. I remember a Gerard Lydon from Surrey in England who visited my guesthouse in July 1968 who wrote 'This has been a most enjoyable holiday and Mr and Mrs O' Driscoll have been the most perfect hosts. If all Ireland is like this then surely this is the Emerald Isle'.

We had Americans staying at Easter in 1969. We had no central heating and they must have been disappointed at this but they still said, 'Though the nights were cold the hospitality was warm and wonderful, I wish we could come back here every year'.

The Reeves family from Carshalton, Surrey, repeatedly visited my guesthouse and we also went to see them. In 1970 she wrote, 'Wonderful food, wonderful holiday, home from home we will be back'.

Sam and Joyce Grundy from Dublin visited us every year for 17 years. These were their comments back in September 1970.

'Super holiday, wonderful friends, can we come back again next year?'

I knew then that I was doing a very good job. I met the odd crank, but in every walk of life you meet people that you cannot satisfy.

Mother heard from a friend that someone that she had known had stayed my guesthouse for a holiday. They said ' they never enjoyed a holiday so much and that the food was wonderful' they also said 'they had made a booking to return the following year'. Mother was completely taken aback about what was said and wondered if it could be true. She could not believe it. The next words that came from her mouth were ' you cannot cook and how could they enjoy a holiday in your house?' Over the 22 years that I ran the guesthouse a void in me had been filled. It made me believe that I was an achiever and that I was not as useless as mother had made me out to be. When I was a child I may have had one foot in the grave. Today I have my two feet above the ground and I can make my own decisions in life and with God at my side I can help people in similar situations.

I wanted to be the best in everything I did and I always said I would never give up. In the middle of my garden there used to stand a lone sunflower. Its face turned towards the sun, bright and cheerful, and that was I, because with God I was getting all the nourishment, guidance and nutrition that I needed. Today I love flowers and I always used to grow them in my garden, especially roses. When I think of my roses now, I remember that they were as beautiful in colour as Heaven. My roses remind me of the rosary and I see them as a precious gift from Our Lady. Maybe that's why I grew roses as I have great love for our lady. Every Rosary that I pray is like giving Our Lady a bouquet of roses.

My Busy Guesthouse

It all started with my husband, and me in this old farm,
Outside in the countryside,isolated to me it was harm.
Inside this farmhouse there was an eerie feeling,f
For my soul and my salvation the fear was no healing,
I tried to change to change things but I thought in vain.
No one listening to me I thought I was going insane.
Inside of me was an unnatural void,
From day to day it grew wide and wide.
Change was important ,it was my agenda,
I decided to be able to see the light through the window.
Darkness had overtaken me at the fasted speed.
The longer I left it the bigger the need.
I sat in silence and decided on my options.
The old ways needed new adaptations
A remoulding challenge for change, I had a great reason,
Brian and decided the idea of a guesthouse was pleasing.
United together we knew could thrive.
And I hoped my world would never again collide.
Money I borrowed to give my house an upgrade.
And in no time I knew the loan would be paid.
In 1967 my doors were open for the first time,I felt like an
old penny that was now shinning,
My guests in large numbers soon started arriving,
This business of mine soon started thriving,
Smiling guests came who had many different cultures,
Never did I have to turn a key in my door,
Nothing ever taken, broken or stolen,
My trust for them from God was a token,
Children laughing and enjoying their play,
Everything they were asked to do they obeyed,
Hard work it took to accomplish this success,
The joy of it all I was Blessed,
My children were so tolerant and dedicated,

For the outside world what a beautiful picture they painted,
They were my support ,which made my business come alive,
Without my family I wouldn't have had the power to strive,
For 22 years I ran my beautiful guesthouse
Inside, I grew like as if I were in a greenhouse,
Lasting friends I made that were so loyal,
Being in their company I felt royal,
I donated my guesthouse as a rehab centre, so I could retire,
I miss the flames from my burning fire,
The memories of it all I store and cherish.
In my mind and heart like treasure,
Having my guesthouse turned my darkness into light,
Now I live day and night,
Happy to have this achievement under my belt,
It's an iceberg of mine that will never melt.

A BOUNCING BABY BOY

Just as on any other day I was carrying on with my work but on this day, for some reason, I did not feel very well. I had a funny feeling that something was wrong and a few days later knew that I was pregnant. I was overjoyed but had a sense of fear that I would not be able to cope.

I knew that I had a lot of stress in my life, partly because I had four children under the age of ten, and wondered if I would get through this pregnancy, as all the others were difficult. I was afraid that it would put my health in jeopardy. I had been told by the doctors not to have another child and now that I was pregnant these words rang in my ears. With my health the way it was I was also afraid to tell Brian because he felt that we had enough children. All during the pregnancy I placed my trust in God but at times it was difficult. I wondered if I died how my children would get by. This took me back to my own childhood and depression overtook me. My children were everything to me and one thing that I did not want was to see them without a mother.

I was proud to look after my four beautiful children because I knew how difficult it was not to have a mother and to be so deprived of love and affection. A dark shadow overtook me like a cloud that was full of rain. For some reason or other it did not shift. I did not want to show my feelings to my family and I did not want to let them know how ill I was. They were all looking forward to the new baby because they knew no differently. My girls asked me every day when the baby would be coming. They were so caring and they kept telling me all through my pregnancy that they would take care of the baby in the same way that they helped me with the guesthouse. I could also see that they were concerned in case I would not pay them attention, which was only natural.

My children were so good in every way and so understanding. I knew that if I told them how unwell I was they might have not been able to cope but I got to a stage eventually when I told Brian. I cried for days and sometimes longed to die because I thought I was going to die anyway. The only thing that gave me the will power to carry on was looking at my four beautiful children.

Eventually I reached a stage when I could hardly walk. I could not climb the stairs and had to sleep downstairs with the end of my bed elevated. When I went back to my doctor he told me what I was expecting to hear, that my life was at risk and so was my baby's if I did not stay in bed for the remainder of my pregnancy. He wanted to admit me to hospital there and then but I fought and asked him if I could stay at home for another few months. I was very lucky that I had met the kindest gynaecologist and had known him since my nursing days. Before I got married I worked in a small private nursing home and this gynaecologist used to send his patients there. The only hope left to me was that I might hold a beautiful baby in my arms that I could love and care for. My children were my heaven and my earth.

Even though the doctor told me to go to bed I was not too happy about the idea. Motivation drove me to get the jobs done and although I had got out of the habit of worrying when I was a teenager I was now back at it again. However I had no choice. I knew that I was treading a dangerous road if I did not do as I was told. I gave advice on the running of the guesthouse to the girls that I had employed and guests were helpful and understanding. Brian was very supportive with the guesthouse but I do not know how he coped with the girls, the children, the cows and myself sick.

After a short while I did have to go to hospital and remained there until I had the baby. The doctor promised to induce me when I was eight months pregnant and just hoped that I would hold on to the child until then. I had a very badly infected, prolapsed womb and was traumatised again because I blamed the abuse of my childhood and the hard work I did in the guesthouse. I started to hate myself inside. You can imagine how uncomfortable the end of my pregnancy was with the elevated bed and the constant pain. It was like being in labour all the time and I was living in a world of darkness. I could not see any light at the end of the tunnel. I was in a state of terror until I had my baby from the realisation that both my baby and I might die and was very relieved when the doctor induced me at eight months. When labour started I had a glimpse of hope and a sense of peace that everything was going to be all right. The nun in charge of the labour ward was very unpleasant but when she saw how ill I was she became kind. I was put under anaesthetic for the delivery and was not very pleased about it as I always liked to be awake and the first to see the baby. However the next morning when I woke up I was told that I had a 7 LB, bouncing, baby boy; he was a bundle of joy and worth all the pain. I was so drained though, that I was not able to hold my baby - all I wanted was rest. When I cuddled him later that day I just felt so happy that we both lived.

In the last couple of days before I had him I was so close to God. I prayed very hard to Saint Anthony to pull me through. My prayers were answered during my time of trial. At this time my longing for God was intense, because the suffering in my life was so great. I loved my little baby with his two big blue eyes looking up at me. He was every mother's dream. They allowed me to go home after eight days but my other children came into the hospital to see me in the meantime. They were so excited - 'what name are you going to give him Mammy? ' I knew already. I was going to put Anthony in his name.

The doctors decided that it was safe for me to go home even though my stitches tore and I was very poorly but I felt myself that I was not well enough. However, alarm bells were ringing in my head that I should go home and look after my children who needed me. There were five now and they were pining for their Mother. Anyway, you can only take so much of hospital life even though I enjoyed seeing other mothers being united with their babies and the sense of closeness I had developed a great friendship with the other patients. The smell of all the disinfectant was a different smell to the fresh air I was used to.

When I went home I was still in a lot of pain, but I was alive. I made it through and I knew in my heart that Jesus would always heal every wound.

Brian loved our little boy and said that he would have 'another little helper for the cows'. Fathers always like to have sons who can share their interests and that was the case with my Brian. My elder son was more like me though and we enjoyed the same things. He was a mammy's boy. Brian said that he was going to train his new son to follow in his footsteps. Soon it would be like Father, like Son. He would no longer be alone in the fields and would have help. Brian was good and caring but at times I felt that he was married to the farm. Having my baby brought Brian and myself closer though, because in a marriage the children are the foundation that makes the relationship stronger.

My ill health continued for a long time after I came home. I was awake at night but could not get out of bed to feed my baby. My eldest little girl, who was nine, used to make up the feeds and change the baby and to this day they are very close. My daughter Nollaig used to get up at night. She was only five years old but she would give him his bottle. We all managed him together and I was lucky that he was healthy and very quiet.

God again came to my rescue. The gynaecologist promised me that he would perform an operation when the baby was six months old. The doctor kept to his word; I had the operation and thank God it was a success. Then my health started to improve and life was wonderful for a few years.

From a seed to a flower

When we were born,
We were like a seed in its shape and form,
Jesus nourished us and gave us our feeds,
He looked after our every need.

Now that the seed has grown into a bud,
Jesus has done for us all He could,
To make us happy as we grow,
In His image we do glow.

The bud now grows into a flower,
And it time for Jesus to use His power,
To shower us with colour as we bloom,
So our scent will be left in every room.

Jesus loves everything as you can see,
From a flower to a tree,
And if He loves these,
What a greater love he has for you and me.

TOGETHER CRUCIFIED

In 1982, disaster really struck my life. I noticed a change in Brian's personality; he lost all interest in working on the farm, and seeing after the cattle. I was very worried, because I felt some of the animals were neglected. He was making no money, and running the farm at a loss and I had to work extra hard in the guesthouse, to rear my children. It was very difficult for my family, as some of then had now reached their teens.

It was torture for my 8-year-old son because he was very close to his father, and all of a sudden Brian stopped showing him love. He could not understand why his father's attitude changed towards him and thought his father had turned against him. Brian mixed up his friends' names when they called to the door looking for him and sometimes passed silly remarks, or teased John in front of them which John found really embarrassing.

As a child, John was very keen on sport, and his father now refused to take him to football matches. He had to rely on neighbours for a lift and then, just about half way through a match, Brian would turn up and refuse to bring him home. John was quite a shy little boy and this caused him great suffering. My husband lost all interest in the family, and how the children were getting on at school or anywhere else.

He used to tell the children that he was not their father, and his attitude changed towards me totally. He refused to give me any money, and he refused to buy any clothes for himself. His personality changed so much it was as if I was married to a different man and at times I felt a stranger in his company. Sometimes he could be his old self, and at other times his mood would change and he would have outbursts of anger for no apparent reason. I used to ask myself whether I was a good wife and wondered if I might be the cause of his anger.

My son Brian Og, was a wonderful support to me during this period, then he emigrated to America, and I felt the bottom had fallen out of my life. Then I noticed that Brian was talking a lot about his childhood; he refused to take me shopping or help out in any way with the children. He was finding it more difficult to manage the farm, so we sold all our cattle, and rented out the land.

Sometimes when I used to talk to him I noticed that he did not understand half of what I was talking about and would interpret it the wrong way and get angry. One night when he was coming home from the local pub, he got lost and it took him hours to find his way home. This upset him very much, because deep down I think he knew something was happening in his life that he had no control over.

I confided in my mother, and she said I should 'get on with it' and that she had been through more than I had. The floodgates of my childhood opened again. It is funny that when you are at your lowest ebb and things go wrong, your whole life comes before you again. It is like the story of your life, and you read it chapter by chapter. This is what used to happen to me, when I knew Brian was ill.

Then I noticed his memory was beginning to fail, and that when he was driving he made mistakes. Sometimes he would get confused, talk about his childhood and start looking for his mother. Every day he would talk about going home. When I tried to explain to him that everything was O.K., and that he was at home, he would get very aggressive, hit me, punch me and sometimes pinch me. I was in denial about his illness, as it was the only way I could cope and told the children that their father was a bit odd, and to ignore his behaviour. I never thought a man in his early fifties would get dementia. I always associated it with elderly people.

Then Mother became very ill with cancer of the spine and I opted to care for her. She was bed-ridden and incontinent and with her commands and orders, it was like a double crucifixion. Now I had Brian to care for, Mother, the guesthouse, the farm and our family. I craved for someone to turn to, to talk things over with. For some reason I kept everything to myself. I was suffering from fatigue and stress, as mother was so difficult. She also had a heart condition, needing to be lifted up in bed a few times during the night. The words she used to use to bring me down when she was sick still haunt me. I then got shingles, and was not able to stay in bed; it was difficult to even get time to go to the doctor. God was very good to me during this stressful period and put beautiful people in my way. I had a very helpful doctor, who was understanding and kind. Then my own health really started to deteriorate and I felt so tired that I could barely cope. Mother became more demanding, as her own health was also failing and I decided to put her into a local hospital, where I knew she would be well cared for. She was angry with me, for putting her into hospital and I felt sorry for her, but I had not the time to grieve over changed circumstances.

Mother was very demanding in the hospital, and the staff found her difficult. She was now in her eighties and was suffering from bedsores. At the end of the day, family is family, blood is thicker than water, and she seemed so unhappy in the hospital that it cut me in two to see her suffering. She died peacefully in 1990 and I was the last of her family to see her alive.

The guests that stayed in my guesthouse were like family and helped me in every way possible. I never told them that I was going through a rough time but I think they knew. Some of them still keep in contact with me, although I closed my guesthouse fourteen years ago.

I knew that Brian loved me, and I tried to relive the happier years. I had a lot of guilt, and I kept saying to myself, 'If only we had done more things together, gone on more holidays and shared more time together before his illness'. He was a loyal friend and a loyal husband. I prayed to God for the grace of acceptance, because I knew that I had to carry on, for the sake of my children.

In 1990 I made a decision to move to town and this was the best move I ever made. We had some wonderful years together, and Brian and myself were never closer. I had some lovely friends and neighbours who were good to me. Sometimes friends can be more helpful than blood relations and those friends were lifelong friends who had done nursing training with me.

Shortly after I moved to town I took Brian to the doctor and he was diagnosed as having Alzheimer's disease. The doctor looked me straight in the eye, and said 'He is not going to get better, but gradually worse'. As I walked up the hill with Brian, hand in hand, the thought came to me that it would be a living death. I grieved for the man I once knew for I now had another child to care for. His memory started to deteriorate more rapidly but the children now began to understand his sickness, and they helped in every way possible. I thanked God that I still had him, and that his physical health was good. We went everywhere together, hand in hand. Eventually he became more aggressive and had to be put on sedation.

He would wander off, and one night he got out of bed about 2 a.m. and, after fully dressing himself, put on his overcoat and shoes. He then went straight back into bed. When I scolded him, he punched me until I started to cry and ask myself, where was God in this? I began to pray, and God gave me peace. Then Brian became incontinent and he had to wear nappies. He used to get very restless at times and when he played with toys he had a particular fascination with keys and used to hide them from me, which I found very frustrating.

I then read a book on Alzheimer's disease, written by a psychiatrist whose husband had the same type of Alzheimer disease, as Brian. She suffered the same as I did, because his personality changed over a period of years before he began to lose his memory. He, too, refused to support her, or spend any money on himself. She then divorced her husband, because she could not accept the change in his behaviour and some years later, when she called to see him, she discovered to her horror that he had Alzheimer's disease. It gave me a greater understanding of Brian's sickness, and helped me to cope.

Brian and myself prayed a lot, and we went everywhere together. We went for walks to the local restaurants, and I did everything I could to make life pleasant for him. He then reached a stage when he did not know the family, or me. One night when Brian was very ill, God gave me a beautiful gift of visions, and I have had this gift ever since.

When Brian was ill the door had to be always locked because he would wander out into the street but one night a lady forgot and, as a result, Brian got out. We notified the guards, who were very kind and helpful to him, during his illness. A young guard even called to my door, and said he would help me in any way he could. When we looked out, to our horror there was no trace of him and the family searched every area in the town, every parked car, and every road out of town. It was a cold, damp night and I knew that if Brian sat down and fell asleep he would get pneumonia. I also knew he was capable of running in front of a car, or running into the nearby river.

I started to pray the rosary, and I asked our lady to work a miracle for me, and to bring him home alive. When I had finished the second rosary, Our Lady spoke to my heart, and told me that Brian was safe, and that she had him in her care. This was about 2 a.m. I found it difficult to convince my family of this, who stayed up all night praying, and searching around the town.

At 8 a.m. a detective called to the door, and he said he had great news for me, " Brian is here and alive and well" but I was so emotional that I could not go to the door. He told me he had crossed a main road, got up behind the man's house and climbed over his garden fence. In the field there was a gap where cattle used to pass from one field, into another. Brian fenced that gap. It must have kept him going all night. Brian had been a farmer and he knew all about fencing-in cattle and I knew Our Lady and Jesus had been with him all night, as he was warm and had no ill effects. We made him comfortable, and he slept for hours afterwards.

In March 1996, he became very ill with a chest infection and never recovered completely. He lost a lot of weight, became very stooped and had a lost look in his eyes. As he became weaker he found it difficult to walk and I decided that he needed hospital care, as it took two people to manage him. Brian was hospitalised for the last 2 months of his life and I found this period very difficult. It was hard to accept that he would never come home and I felt it was worse than a death. Although he could not tell me how he felt I knew that he was unhappy, and this broke my heart. God took him to his eternal home on the 11th of June 1996, where he will suffer no more pain, a place where there are no tears. I hope to join him some day. We had 33 happy years together, even if he was sick for half that period.

God blesses the person who patiently endures testing. Afterwards they will receive the crown of life that God has promised, to those who love Him. (James 1 verse 12)

I now walk down the road of life, but I am not alone. My husband is gone and I know he is with God. My childhood tears are now dried up, and flowing is the precious blood of Jesus in my life.

He handed me life, and gave me a chance. All the years gone by, He has enhanced. I wake up every morning, sometimes sad, But thinking of Jesus makes me glad. I put my hands in the air and welcome the Lord as my saviour, Because in my life he has shown me favour. With Jesus, I too, was once crucified My life is a testimony for those who need to believe. With God's help everything in your life will come right, because God can give you great insight. So you will be like a bird, you can fly free.

ALZHEIMERS DISEAESE

Oh, what an illness, many diseases occur throughout our lives,
We do our best to get up, keep going and strive,
We may bear wounds and burdens, that are physically deep,
But if we lose our minds there is no life to seek.
Alzheimer's is a progressive illness, that changes you over time,
You forget everything; it destroys your mind,
You see things differently; you go backwards and become aggressive,
Your life is not like the one you used to live.
It causes you to lose your independence and you look with a
different colour through the window.
You become like a child, lost, and feel alone,
And inside you do not feel yourself at home.
As time passes, this illness keeps progressing ,
It is a hard illness, without any resting.
No freedom, no choices, you can no longer make decisions,
You forget things and life has a different vision.
People's names you forget, especially your family,
Through the eyes of a child you now see.
Hand in hand, everywhere you have to be followed,
The person you were once, is now gradually being swallowed.
Harder and harder it gets for family, with Alzheimer's,
Because you always have to be left with a minder.
Understanding this illness is a hard one to grasp,
It is a mighty blow, for how long it lasts,
Once it sets in, it can last for over twenty years.
The family has to carry the burdens and fears.
Praying against Alzheimer's can break the chain of this disease,
And into that person, God's
Peace will flow like a breeze.
The illness that was once in the family
Chain will cease and the love of God
Inside you will be released.

OUR LADY'S ROSE GARDEN

Lord Jesus pick me a flower from your mother's rose garden, which is glowing like a shower. Make it an everlasting rose. Make it bring life to lighten my foes. Let it bring blessings and graces, and into my life bring very special faces. Make it never die, and always be a gift from Our Lady on high. Make it teach me to love, as it showers from above, glowing and growing, like a flower in a bud. Just like a cover on Our Lady's hood. Let this little rose of mine shine, shine shine. Let it always be my flower, and always be my favourite line. Let it always have beauty and always make me happy, so let this little rose of mine, that showered from heaven be my favourite song, and my favourite tune just like the sun and the moon. So pick me my petition and make it a mission never to forget me and always be with me.

Amen

HE THE CAPTAIN AND I THE SAILOR

In 1992 we decided to sell our farm as Brien had reached an advanced stage in his illness. We donated our guesthouse and some of the land as a rehabilitation centre for teenager drug addicts and alcoholics. When you walk hand in hand with Jesus you must always be prepared for opposition. ' If they persecuted me, they will persecute you also' I was unprepared for the opposition which I had to face at that time and Brien been so ill I had to face it on my own. All the neighbours whom I lived close by for 27 years opposed me. They called to my home in town and were very rude and angry towards me. One man called to my guesthouse and said I would be the cause of the school closing down and to reconsider my course of action. They tried to manipulate me, with the auctioneer to sell my guesthouse with the land and by another run down property to be used as a drug treatment centre I in intended it for.

I really came up against neighbours whose tongues were on fire with anger and their hearts full of envy and greed. We should always use our tongues with love, hope and peace. Love should always be our tool as it conquers all evil. It gives hope to the poor helps the lonely and teaches the greedy. We have no right to hate, if you love, love will follow you all the days of your life. Love never hurts anyone. It costs nothing to be kind and always live in peace with our neighbours and us. We should rise above everything with love and think of Our Lord arms outstretched for you on the cross when love is against you. As Christians we should be the symbols of love, hope and peace to everyone. We should never give up hope when people are against us, because ' when God is for you who can be against you'

Thank God this centre has helped a lot of young people. The Minister for Health opened it. Young people have given their testimonies how they were released from the scourge of drug abuse and alcohol and how they got a chance to further their education and see that life is worth living again. Some of those young people felt they had nobody to turn to and felt they were at the end of the road because drugs and drink had taken control of their lives. Thank God their lives have turned around and they no longer feel stressed and hopeless but are now in full control of their lives.

PRAYERS FOR DRUG ADDICTS

Lord Jesus come and reveal yourself to drug addicts and draw them into your love. Help them to see you as a consolation and not the drugs they are taking. Counsel them off the drugs and their suicidal tendencies so they can start again and see you for who you really are, and how good the world is.

Remove the feeling of addiction form their head and the taste of evil from their mouth. Built the missing part in their lives with your love, peace and patience's. Keep inspiring them so they can live without drugs. Help their families to be patient with them and never give up hope.

Lord lightens the darkest parts of their souls with your fire flame of love. Break the bondage's and break the power of the evil one for so long infested their life.

Lord Jesus we make our prayer known to you for drug addicts through Christ Our Lord

Amen

My extended family

I have a great love for drug addicts, I can somehow feel their pain. I prayed with a boy called David who was into drug abuse, alcohol abuse and as a result of the drugs he was taking, his wife was subject to beatings verbal abuse and constantly living in fear. When I prayed with him, God touched him powerfully and he has never taken drugs since. That happened two years ago. I pray everyday for the drug addicts who visit my garden. I call them my extended family. I also pray that their families will live in hope, and that Jesus will give them sufficient strength to cope. ' As Paul said I can do all things through Christ who strengthens me'

THE TEN COMMANDMENTS

The Ten Commandments are important for our growth with God. They are there to teach us obedience and honour Christ the King. God is greater than our heart and he knows all things. The reason why I do not get what I ask is because I do not keep the commandments. It is important to keep in line with the commandments. The commandments are the foundation of God as well as love.

The First Commandment

I am the Lord your God you shall not have strange God's before me.

When God says this he does not want us to put anything before Him, Our eternal Father. Some people see money as their God and the saying goes without reason. The love of money is the root of all evil. When we choose God to be for us we must clear the path of anything else, such as false worship. (Worshipping people that are not God) Occult practices that are not of God, Tara cards, fortune telling etc. Jesus says ' You cannot serve God and mammon' Mt 6:24.

The First commandment then states that believing in God gives us Hope in him and that we must love Him with all our heart above all else.

Remember God ids the divine physician. People put such great faith in hypnoththeraphy, Reiki Healing, Reflexlogy and acupuncture.

All these practices are all new age while a lot of people have faith in them. There healings are only short term going against

God is a grave sin. We were given the ten commandments to obey, they are there for a purpose.

The Second Commandment

Thou shalt not take the name of the Lord thy God in Vain

God is the Father the giver of life and the creator of all mankind. He is the truest God and only God of worship. People today do not respect God the way they should and they take his name in vain. More so his son than any one else. They use his name to curse and swear, so morally wrong. When you are made and brought into the world Jesus did not curse at you but gave you a name. He called you his previous child and did so with delight. People need to have more respect for Jesus as Jesus redeemed us and set us free, if Jesus did not rise from the dead (our faith would be in vain)

Vain should not be used where God is concerned as Jesus rose from the dead. By dying he destroyed our dead and by rising restored our lives. Lord Jesus come in glory. Anger is from the devil and when people get cross and lose self-control they take Jesus name in vain. Self control is a gift from God, man is in control of what he says. Jesus sacrificed his whole life to save us sinners.

We were the dust on the road and God breathed life into us. He gave us his precious son royally to be one of us. How can be turn around and swear and use the name of God and Jesus, which is morally wrong. Jesus won victory over the devil 2000 years ago, but yet people that are involved in oiga boards and magical arts and cursing in the name of Jesus and trying to destroy his good name.

Jesus always conquers evil as God is stronger than evil. People using Jesus name in vain just like the devil is cowards. The devil gets other people to do his dirty wrong and destroys the image of Jesus face. Turn to God today and reprimand yourself to do good. Just as you get it wrong sometimes gives you no authority to swear at Jesus and take his Name in vain as if he does not exist. Treat him as a God of the living and not of the dead.

' You shall worship the lord your God and him only shall you serve' Deuteronomy.

' O Lord our God how glorious is your name in all the earth' Psalm 8

The Third Commandment.

Remember that thou keep holy the Sabbath day

It upsets God so much that people turn away from His church and they are so rebellious and angry towards Him and His church. People must realise that the church is the body of Christ, his body and Blood. People can be as angry as they want towards leaders because they can get it wrong, but nobody should ever criticise God. People should pray for their leaders and their church. The time has come where nobody wants to go to church our confession.

' Every Christian should avoid making unnecessary demands on others that would hinder them for observing the Lord's Day'

People can be ashamed of their religion, which is sad because at the end of the day we all serve the one God.

If only governments knew the power of prayer and knew the inside of God's heart and the fulfilling meaning of Christ, they would change, they would look beyond greed and their own big name. They would see the best in every person and help every one more, like the homeless, the sick, the drug addicts, the prisoners and all the poor people. A lot of money is spent on campaigning for elections, Why can't this kind of money be spent on bringing the good news of God to people and to teach them about his love and hope.

We are living in a time where there is a lot of corruption, but the greater the sinner the greater the Mercy. There is more sin in the world now than ever before, so the hand of God is stronger now and more merciful. So now is the time to repent and turn back and realise there is another leader beyond them. Every leader has a role, every role is important for society so everyone should pray for their leader that they do right. People must pray for priest and for vocations so more people will turn to be priests and live up to their commitments to god, it can be all done through prayer.

Just go to Medjugorje for one week and see how many priests say mass in one day and how beautiful the peace is there. People there have a wonderful gift of faith. Their hearts are changed from hearts of stone to hearts of gold.

We should thank God for all the beautiful apparition of his mother through out the world that still gives us the hope to live on. It is not alone Medjugorje that brings about this beautiful change but other places where our Lady has appeared and people trust in God.

The Fourth Commandment .

Honour thy father and thy mother

We should honour our father and mother and respect out elders. We should trust in them that they know best. We should respect our parents and listen and learn from them. We should pray with our families because the family that prays together stays together. God enlightens our parents to help us when we pray. It is hard for some children because they do not have parents, but they can honour people that are their guardians with some respect if they can.

While no parents are perfect, all parents have their children's interests at heart. While on the road of life their are many different people some are nice some are unkind and some of them are beyond this world in their ways and in their holiness. Some children cannot confide in their parents because their parents might get it wrong and be unkind to their children, but the children can turn to God. They still have the eternal Father and Mother that will be there forever. God will stretch out his hand for them and bring them into the light. So for the children of the world God is with you day and night and all through your life until eternity. Even if you do not know a prayer talk to god he understands. He numbered you and called you his own, a child of God.

For parents it is important that they pray for guidance about their children so they can bring them up the best possible way, and if not God will send someone else to help because not all parents have it easy. Prayer is a solution to all problems. Jesus understands family, as he was a child himself. Ask Jesus to be the centre of your life in your thoughts and in your heart and ask him to teach your children the power of prayer. To all families and parents give your children the foundation of prayer and example to other children.

Teach them to love and never condemn because children become like those who they live with. You only get one chance at been a parent in a child's life, so it is important to do it right. There are a lot of unhappy adults in the world today that had an unhappy childhood and are broken people today. God can heal all broken people if they turn to God. There is nothing God can not do. As Paul said 'I can do all things through Christ who strengthens me'

The greatest gift you can give a child is prayer and faith, as it will last them everyday of their life. It will sow a seed in their hearts that will bloom and while it is hard to be good parents all the time because life is hard the way things are in the world. Just do your best that's all God wants you to do. Parents are responsible for the education of their children to make them responsible adults and future parents themselves.

The Fifth Commandment

You shall not kill.

It is so sinful to take the life of another human being, whatever the reason God is the only one who has the right to give
and take life. There are different ways of killing people, you can
kill a person by spreading bad rumours about a person, whether
true of false taking away a person character. Scandal is always
sinful.

Abortion is taking the life of the unborn child, which cannot defend itself. The child is so vulnerable and has nobody to
speak for him. Abortion destroys the mother, she has terrible
feeling of guilt and regret and this lives with her for the rest of
her life. It will be a grieving, like a death for her.

' Before I found you in the womb I knew you'

Another form of abortion is the morning after pill. Life begins from the moment of conception, if only mothers knew how
the morning after pill could damage their health. The coil is
also wrong it. When contraceptive pill is given at a very young
age. Static have proven that it can cause cancer of the cervix

The people, who carried out these terrible acts of abortion,
are taking the right of another human being to life. At the end
of the day it is a job for them. Ireland has been a wonderful
country not to legalised abortion but only God knows how long
it will last with all the new laws coming in.

Euthanasia is the putting an end to a person's life that suffers
from a terminal illness or where they think there is no hope at
all. It is an easy way out for the person who is ill, as they think
they are a burden to themselves and their families. The family
think they are doing an act of kindness to end the suffering of
a relative. Euthanasia is legalised in some countries, in these
countries the elderly live in fear.

Murder is a deadly sin in all its forms, the body dies but they cannot murder the soul. Pray for people who commits murder and pray for the victim's families and their ongoing grief.

Prayer can change everything. It's important that the Irish pray that abortion and euthanasia be not legalised as it would cause a lot of trouble. Leave life in God's hands because he is the creator and he knows what is best for each person.

There is a motion for every murder, so its important people pray to control their anger. An eye for an eye and a tooth for a tooth for a tooth is not what Jesus taught us. Jesus said turn the other check and forgives the unforgivable. Love your enemies. Love never hurts, hatred never comes from god. Love is beautiful as it comes from God.

The Sixth Commandment

Do not commit Adultery

It is important that we listen to God as he puts us on the right path. If you listen to the eternal father from the beginning you would not commit sin. A man must keep his vows of his marriage and so must his wife. He should be loyal to his wife everyday that follows from the day he got married. He shall love his wife with his whole body, soul, mind and spirit and his wife should be the same to her man.

Whatever people God joins together in marriage should stay together as they become one in God. It is important to be pure when married and to be bonded to one another in prayer. When a man or women goes outside his marriage vows they commit adultery. It is abusing the gifts that God gave them and it is causing them to sin against their own body. It is also lack of respect for other parties that are involved and the trust is broken. It's important to be honest in a marriage and not be deceitful. If a marriage were happy, adultery would not exist. It is important people that are joined together in marriage pray together and stay together. Because what God gives in a marriage the couples should be satisfied. Better a man and women be pure and chase before they get married. Some people are single and stay single but commit adultery in their own way even if they do not have a partner. They become lustful and sleep around. They have lack of respect for their bodies and others. The man and women must learn to say no matter how tempted they become.

You must not let your heart govern your head, you must let your head govern your body, behaviour and actions. Pornographic videos are against God, as well as blue movies and bad books. Pro- creation is a gift from God for married couples and should only be used in marriage. Sex is not a game you play around with which can lead to many diseases such as HIV Clamedia, Herpes and many more that are not even known. Protect yourself from these diseases and the terrible effect they can have on people.

The path of God will never put you wrong. Never worry and try to live a life of holiness. Man and women can offer up their bodies to Jesus Christ the Saviour.

Girls must dress modestly because it offends Our Lady in this century because they can be the cause of a man becoming aroused. Girls must play their part in behaving properly towards men and not be flirting. Our Lady said most who died in the 2nd world war who went to hell went there because of sins against the flesh.

Boys must also behave proplery towards girls. Homo sexually is wrong. Being gay is not sinful it is when they commit sexual acts, man with man and women with women. It is wrong to make jokes about gay people because they should not be judged. Jesus said judge not and you shall not be judged. Pray against temptation as god is stronger than evil. Fornication is very sinful, polygamy is a grave sin against the dignity of marriage. God blesses the people that he joins together and gives them wonderful gifts throughout their life together. Children are the foundation of all love in any marriage.

Incest is a grave sin, It does a lot of harm to the person that is effected by it, and it breaks the trust in the family. A trial marriage is also wrong no matter how fashionable it is today.

Our bodies are the temples of the Holy Spirit. If God lives within us God has the key and we must respect our bodies.

Man and women must learn to control their action in sexual behaviour and they should ask God help them not to be tempted in anyway or do anything immoral which is a sin against the flesh.

The Seventh Commandment

You shall not steal

Stealing is a moral sin, You should not take what does not belong to you. Stealing goes with greed, wanting more than what you have. Sometimes it is because someone has addiction, othertimes because someone is poor and have nothing. It does not matter what the motive was behind the act there is no excuse for stealing.

Can you imagine the person you stole from and how upset they would be if their life savings are stolen or something which has a sentimental value. Just imagine how awful they would feel. Put yourself in their shoes if they stole from you how would you feel. Stealing causes a lot of hurt and there is broken trust. Would 'nt. it be a lovely country if everyone could leave their doors open and there would be no locking up of anything. It would be such a free country. Normally stealing happens between people who know one another. They spot what is in each other's house that's what sets the temptation going. It is terrible that family members can not trust each other because of this addiction. Money is the most common kind of theft. Everyone should think twice before they steal because it is a very important commandment.

It is actually how much you steal it is what you steal from family members or others because you will not be trusted again.

THE TEARS I CRIED, HE DRIED

If you rob from strangers you will not know the consequences of how it would effect them because they could be poor people. Normally a lie goes with thieving as they deny what they have done. Once you become a thieve you go on to steal bigger things. Because if you get away with it once you will think you will get away with it again, but thieve do get caught at some stage. There are a lot of sad faces in prisons today because of stealing.

Think before you steal because one day it will be too late and you could end up behind bars. So turn to God today and ask him to help you fight this addiction if you have this problem and ask him to provide what you need and you then will not have to steal. Trust in the Lord's power he can do anything for you can help you change

' Neither thieves nor robbers nor the greedy will inherit the kingdom of God'

The Eighth Commandment

You shall not bear false witness against your neighbour's

This is a commandment that teaches us that we should love our neighbour as ourselves, which is repented in the bible so many times. This commandment means we should not lie or deceive our neighbours our take their character away. These are people who live beside us every day of every year. They are our friends in time of need. They keep us company and come to visit us when we are ill. They teach us to love and to be g generous to one another. It would be a lonely place without our neighbours, as we would have no place to go in time of need. Our neighbours should be our friends and people we can trust. It is the trust is broken that's when problems occur. Gossip is the thing that ruins everything between neighbours

This is what destroys relationships. In Ireland today families move because they can not get on with their neighbours.

Some neighbours are nasty to one another and enjoy fighting and making a scene.

Revenge is a big factor, because families play one off against the other, by lying and telling stories One of the commonest problems that causes fights today is people having affairs with their neighbour, then this causes the families to break up. This is only a small portion of deceit among neighbours not getting on, but there are many more reasons.

So start today and do a kind act for your neighbour and treat them as your friends because you will never know when you might need them and at least they will be there for you. Do not build up any barriers against your neighbours because you must give every one a chance. You then will have many friends in your life.

Prov.12. Verse. 22 ' The Lord hates liars but is pleased with these who keeps his word'

The Ninth Commandment

You shall not covet your neighbours wife

It is very wrong to do immoral things in your marriage and to commit adultery with your neighbours. Befriend your neighbours in a neighbourly love and not a lustful love. You need your neighbours as your friend in time of need nothing worse than living in fear incase your husband or wife finds out what you are up to with your neighbour. Trust in God to find satisfaction in him not in desires and sexual fantasies.

Have cop on and listen to God and what he has in store for you which are only good. If you are not satisfied in your own relationships go to a marriage counsellor and work out your difficulties instead of getting bored and going elsewhere. Some people desire and temptations are worse than appetites and have no control over them. Man is cauterised in public how he behaves as well as a woman. In public what you hear is what you believe instead of seeing and believing.

It is a sin against the body to do anything that is not of God. Only if you knew the joy that awaits you in heaven you would not be caught up in earthly things.

Start a new life today with God and change your old ways. Put on the wineskins and make a new start. Because there is a long road a head in life and do the best you can. If you have problems turn to God and he will give you answers and lead you not into temptation but deliver you from evil.

The Tenth Commandment

You shall not covet our neighbour's goods.

This is an important commandment, It teaches us all to be happy with what we have and not envy our friends or neighbours with what they have got. Just ember different things make different people happy. When you envy your friends have in life if it is money or property, may not be the cause of their happiness. Jealousy another form of envy, What causes jealously is another cause of our insecurities, which build up in us from the past. If we were happy people we would not be jealous. Jealously is a word that is commonly felt by the poor or people who have very little.

There is no need for anyone to be jealous as God has given us all enough to go through life. Spiritual gifts are much more important than material gifts. Jealously and envy cause people to steal because they begrudge another person what they have. It also causes people to sin and to be tempted to do a lot of wrong things like damaging people's property.

Turn to God today and ask him to deliver you from your temptation and to fill you with his love. He will release you and give you joy and fulfil his happiness in you so you do not have to envy or be jealous of anyone anymore. He will give you a heavenly peace if you trust in him, which will be nicer than anything you could ever wish for.

Taken in Scotland in 1960

Taken in 1958 with a group of friends at a hospital dance

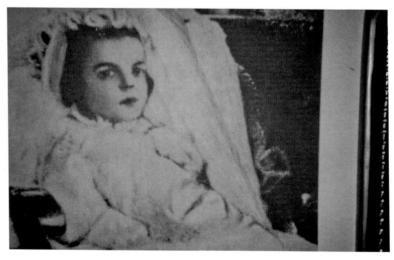

Little Nellie of Holy God

Taken when I worked in Scotland in 1960

Brian and I on our Wedding day, October 7th 1963

Brian and I

A photograph of my guesthouse, Ahiohill House, taken in 1991. It is now known as Cara Lodge and serves as a rehabilitation centre for recovering drug addicts.

My garden before it was made into a Holy Garden

My garden as it is now

Entrance to the garden

Some recent visitors to the garden, 2010

Some of the grandchildren

Taken when Brian was ill

Brian Og O'Driscoll's Wedding in Boston in 1989

A family portrait at our daughter Lucy's Wedding on 7ᵗʰ
October 1993. It was also our 30ᵗʰ Wedding anniversary.
I had both joy and sorrow on this day, as Brian had now
reached an advanced stage of illness and we had some diffi-
culty trying to persuade him to attend the ceremony

A family portrait at our daughter Nollaig's Wedding in May 1994

John's Wedding in the gulf of Mexico in 2009

Brian and I in 1968

BRIAN'S DEATH

When Brian died I felt a void in my life. It was like part of me had died with him. I once again became empty. I was all alone and I was haunted by the far that I would not be able to cope. The same question I asked as a child, on my wedding day and on the day my fifth child was born. All my life when something traumatic happens I end up questioning myself why? Why? Why? But I know now it was all part of God's plan.

There is time for growing, a time for harvesting, a time to be born and a time to die. Brian had done his journey on earth and I prayed he would make the final journey home to heaven. I was devastated at Brian's death. It was like a sudden death. I had known for years that this day would come but you can never be prepared for a death. You may think you are.

The shock does not hit the system until you know your loved one is gone. You never know what something is until it's gone that was me. I was happy that Brian was taken out of his suffering. On the other hand I was angry that he had developed Alzheimer's because it had eventually led to his death.

The day that I got the phone call that he was dying, I went to the hospital and he died with me at his side. At least I knew that he spent his last moments with me. I chose my husband for love and him I loved.

My life has moved on and still I miss him. I cried for months after. I had so many questions yet I had no answers. Why my husband? Had I not gone though enough in life? It was like the storytale of my life was been recycled. My loneliness as a child and now the loneliness again. When I was a child I climbed the mountain step by step and now I felt that I had ended back up where I started.

I said to God why go backwards this hour of my life. I knew when I married Brian that it was for better or worst sickness and in health. I thought I would go first not Brian. Because of the bad health I suffered. I thought I would be in someone's arms for the rest of my days. I pined that this did not happen. I also pined for my love lost husband. The memory of him has never died. And I hold them in my heart because they are part of me.

But God has a plan for each of us. I did not realise that He had a plan for my life when Brian was gone. A plan to use me as His tool to do His work. If Brian was here it would not be the same as Brian is in heaven helping me and he could not be in a better place. If Brian was here with me I would not have the time to take care of him and do the work I am doing now. I don't even have a moment now because all my time is spent helping God's people in various ways.

When Brian died I was lonely and upset. God had a plan I for me something I never thought would happen. I am not empty I am full of all the gifts of the Holy Spirit. Even though I am alone I have everything that anyone could ask or live for.

When God is part of me I am fulfilled. Even though I got many opportunities to be in other relationships when Brian died. When I got married I said Brian was the only man for me and I suck to these words. Mother's words rang out in my ears the day that Brian died 'You will never marry' I knew I had fulfilled every vow I had made to Brian on our wedding day.

In a way I was proud because I survived a marriage and lived it through. Brian is now dead eight years and the time has passed quickly. I still miss him very much. I go to mass every day and afterwards I visit the cemetery. I get great peace and comfort at his grave. I know one day I will be united to him, which will be eternal. I know our hearts will be burning with the fire of God's love for each other.

My children also miss their father very much. Step by step they have gone through the grieving process and have accepted it. We are strong for each other and that's what makes a family. We are all members of the family of God. After Brian's death only for the comfort and the support that each member of my family gave me I would not have survived. To them I am ever grateful.

My Mother in Her Final Years

After I had made a life for myself and settled down, and my children were teenagers, my Mother was getting old and there came a time when she could no longer care for herself. I opted to take her, to mind her and look after her. Despite all that my Mother had done to me in life, I forgave her, and I couldn't see her going into a home. I knew she could no longer take care of herself as she had cancer of the spine and a heart condition. She stayed with me until she became so ill that she had to go to hospital. Living with my Mother I felt as if I was a child again, and that I was under her control, even though I was in my own home. She was the same bully as she always had been and I felt as if I was under her command to do whatever she asked. My life seemed no longer my own, it was like being back home in a cage.

My Mother was one of the most difficult people ever, to live with. I had enough on my hands trying to cope with guests in my home and trying to make a living. I had a sick husband and a sick mother to take care of. I had hardly any time to see my children, even though they were teenagers and they still needed me. My youngest was only 13 years old and he needed a lot of attention, as he was trying to come to terms with his father's illness. I found it so hard trying to balance my life. My mother never seemed to appreciate my looking after her. She was very disrespectful to my children and sometimes you would wonder whose house it was. I did my best to make her happy but with no thanks and I could never do enough. I could never understand, after all she had done to me, why I took her on when she was old. When I left home as a teenager I had been delighted with my freedom.

Even when I was looking after her she was never respectful to me the way I was respectful to her, and that was the way all my life. When other relations would come and visit she wanted me out of the room and would get as excited as if it was the

Queen she was meeting. When visitors came to see her, Mother had smiles on her face which she never had for me, no matter what I did. It was like a million pounds to her to see her family. She never appreciated me and I always clashed with her. She could never understand my personality because it was so different from hers. I was like the brazen child she did not want, or the maid she treated me as, when I was young. I was still the outcast. She would send me out of the room in my own home when other relations and cousins visited her. Not only had she taken over my life as a child, she had now taken over my home. I was a bit of dirt again.

My children were afraid of her because they saw the way she upset me and they often wished that she were out of their home. I prayed for peace in the house so that there would be no more clashing. I often asked myself the question, 'why doesn't God answer my petitions'? Sometimes, I noticed when my sisters or relatives came to visit her that she had more hatred for me after they left. Looking after my Mother was the work of 3 men, because she was very ill, and needed a lot of care. I don't know how my poor children coped with having someone so cranky all the time. They even helped to care for her and did it with reverence to please me. Time and time again I said to myself, will my health ever stand up to it as she needed a lot of care at night as well as during the day.

As you can see, my Mother's and my own relationship were always one of hatred from beginning to end, more hate at times than love. What she held against me I do not know but what I do know, as a result of what I suffered, is that, it is hard being a mother. Thank God I broke the chain of what happened in my childhood, as I hope what happened to me then will never happen to my own children. It is important to think ahead in life, and to take responsibility for every action and every word we say, so that we don't make life difficult for another human being. We should be controlled by the spirit of God, and not by mankind.

I looked after Mother for 2 years until I could no longer care for her, as my own health started to deteriorate from being up a lot at night with her. I put every effort into looking after her but she got very bitter towards me for putting her into hospital and could not forgive me for doing this to her. She was a very proud person and did not like being put there. She did not change in the hospital either. She was very demanding and the staff found her difficult to cope with. Seeing her suffering in the hospital tore me apart, because I still loved my mother. When the staff were rude to her it caused me great pain even though I knew she was difficult. The greatest gift anyone could ask for is a relation or a parent to die a happy death. I was very grateful to God that my Mother was deeply into prayer before she died.

A LOVE THAT BE SO PROFOUND

A love between mother and daughter should always be unique.
But for me it was nothing, but bleak.
I sought for my mother's attention.
But when I did it was always detention
As cold as ice like something out of a deep freeze
At times I wanted to give her a shaking up and a big squeeze
To see if she would change and treat me as her child
She was harsh and her words were never mild
She was a person that there was no reasoning
When I was upset there was no easing
Everything I did for her had to be pleasing.
When she wanted me I was like the flower in seasoning
I had to protect her little secrets I was like a little warrior
Helping her as a maid I was her courier,
Where was that bond that should have been so profound?
I always wanted to hear words of love in sound
Born for her pleasure to give her glory,
She controlled my life and that is the story

WORDS IN MY EARS

In my ears, today, I can hear words again and again and they are my mother's words, the ones that brought me down. Because I found Jesus they are not as strong but are still very invasive in my life. If you do not want someone in your company you can walk away and forget about them, but these words speak to me a lot and I cannot walk away from them because they are now part of me. It can be very frustrating when I cannot get them out of my mind.

You can try and shut out such words but if a situation arises, such as an argument or a disagreement, your whole life is brought into the situation. Instead of looking at something the way it is and its real value, you make a big issue out of it and it eventually becomes like a storm in your brain. Then you explode because you are not able to cope, and people stand around wondering what the hell is going on as it was about something so minor. My own life could have gone either way, good or bad. I could not detach myself from the parts of me that were in pain when I was in the company of other people. Pain was my package and I grieved then, because those others did not know or understand, and when you are in pain you analyse everything everyone does.

So, if you like, you could say that my punishment was never-ending. Unless you take the grit out of water it will not be safe to drink and I was re-cycling my pain and drinking that dirty water because I did not know any differently. That's why people have a tendency to stay away from those who are broken in case they might get hurt themselves. They are afraid of being burdened with other people's problems when everyone today feels they have enough of their own.

Jesus said, 'If you die to yourself you will have a new life in Him'. That's why we must die to our past so we shall be able to live tomorrow. Jesus also said that, if someone is lukewarm He will spit him out of His mouth`. We are being the same as lukewarm but Jesus will not spit us out because it is a different situation. We are half-hopeful and half in the dark, and, in the dark clouds, hope is something we cannot see.

We live in a self-pitying world, saying, ' poor me, why me'? All this self-pity eventually leads to self-obsession and people can become very self-centred through no fault of their own. They think the world owes them a living and they put all their anxieties, tension and stress on to other people, like their family and friends. When their families and friends do not listen they can go into a deep depression. Depression is like a flat tyre; when the tyre has no air, it cannot be motivated or go anywhere, it has no energy. When it has air it can do anything and move forward. When we have problems we should detach ourselves and hand them over to Jesus, saying, ' now You, Jesus, take control of my life'. Otherwise, we would drive ourselves insane with thoughts going around and around in our heads, and we would imagine things that are not there at all and make ourselves more afraid.

It's funny that people who are hopeful can look at things in the right way, and not waste all their energy like some people do. The reason being, I suppose that hope is from God and depression and sadness come from Satan. All people who suffer in life use the same thought patterns and unless they break the habit they will be left in the dark. That's why the healing of memories is so important. When people are healed they may remember the things that happened but the pain will be gone and if someone talks to them about their past they will be able to share it with them. Many people today have been helped and they go around giving their own testimony of how God healed their memories so that it was possible to move forward in His grace.

If we live in God he will live in us and He can help us get over everything. Just imagine that you have a problem and think of it as a tennis ball; give it a hard belt with a tennis racket so that it will not come near you or affect you. If Jesus is living in you you'll have no worries because Jesus is the same today, yesterday and forever. Jesus knows what you are going through and He understands it. Jesus knew what was ahead of Him before He was crucified and he still reached out in love and forgot about Himself. I found Jesus in time before my life was eaten away and I look at things in a hopeful way because with Jesus there is no other way.

He the Captain and I the sailor

Part 2

In 1990 I had to make the biggest decision I had ever made in the 27 years that I was married to Brian. My husband Brian had become very ill and had now reached the late stages of Alzheimer's Disease. Over the previous 27 years I had been unable to leave the countryside and now this was my opportunity – the one and only one I would ever get because I was now making decisions on my own. I had spent the last seven years caring for Brian and running the guesthouse. During this time we had grown close and it had been no easy job. I was in the heart of isolation and I said "enough is enough". I was living with a man who was very ill and I knew that it was only a matter of time before he would go to God.

Brian was just like a child and I could not take my eyes off him. I was on the lookout for a nice house that would accommodate my family in a convenient location and I prayed to Our Lady to pick one of her choice. We found one in a lovely area and although I am a very indecisive person, the minute I entered this house I could feel a wonderful peace. I knew instantly that this was the house that I wanted. We looked at it on a Saturday and paid our deposit the following Monday morning.

We decided to sell the farm. The local people were very interested and some were amazed that a successful businesswoman like myself would get up and leave. They did not realise that I had good reasons for doing so. I dedided to donate my guesthouse as a treatment centre for drug addicts and alcoholics but when the news got out, all hell broke loose amongst locals. I was not prepared for the opposition I had to face at that time. With Brian being so ill I had to face it on my own but when you walk hand in hand with Jesus you must be prepared for opposition. As it says in scripture: "If they persecuted me, they will persecute you also." All the neighbours whom I had lived close to for 27 years were very angry and tried to stop me in my tracks. Rumours went out that I was having drug addicts who would be using needles.

One man called to my guesthouse and said that I would be the cause of the school closing down and to reconsider my course of action. He tried to manipulate Brian and as Brian was so ill this was very hurtful to me. Groups of people called to my house, were rude and abusive towards me and said that those teenagers would be never made welcome in the area. They said they did not want them to do their shopping in the local shop. One lady asked me how she would cope if she met them on the road while she was walking her dog. They even went to the auctioneer to see if he would ask me to sell my guesthouse with the land and to buy another run down property, as any old building would do as a treatment centre.

I really came up against neighbours whose tongues were on fire with anger. We should always use our tongues with love, hope and peace. Love should always be our tool as it conquers all evil. It gives hope to the poor, helps the lonely and teaches the greedy. We have no right to hate. If you love, love will follow you all the days of your life for love never hurts anyone. It costs nothing to be kind and always live in peace with our neighbours. We should rise above everything with love and think of Our Lord's arms outstretched when life is against us.

I never realised, I would come up against such opposition. I thought it would be like any normal sale. I never thought their behaviour and actions could be so aggressive. I felt I had done a good deed in donating my guesthouse as a treatment centre for drug addicts. Different rumours spread around and some of them became quite bizarre.

The neighbours said that just because I had made my mind up to move did not mean they too should have to move, and this is what they felt they would have to do, if a drug treatment centre opened up. They thought the fact that drug addicts would move into their community would mean a loss of business.

The neighbours were also afraid their children would be attacked by the drug addicts. They did not seem to comprehend that these inmates would be placed in a supervised unit. The

THE TEARS I CRIED, HE DRIED

rumour that came back to me was that I would be the person in charge of the addicts and they would run wild in the neighbourhood. It was even perceived that I would condone drug-abuse. My idea was that sick young people would get treatment and could live a healthy life following therapy.

It was also said that I would be fleeing the area and going to town, making it seem as if I would be turning my back on them. It was looked on as a selfish act.

A very well known Cork youth-priest was going to take charge of the unit. He was well known for doing excellent rehabilitation work with young addicts. I arranged for this priest to have a public talk with the neighbours and tell them about the good work that he was going to do. This greatly helped to allay the fears of the people in the locality. They were surprised to hear that none of the young people used needles, or caused trouble. He assured them he would be in complete charge. And he also involved by telling them if they would like to help he would be open to such offers.

After some time the attitude of the people began to change. They showed great compassion. The people of the community allowed those at the centre to integrate into local life, in particular into the local sporting organisations. Their eyes became opened and they began to view things differently. The locals began to lose their hard feelings. They understood that none of the young people were allowed to leave the building, unsupervised.

Drug-users in the main come from broken or dysfunctional homes where they cannot cope. The reason they take drugs is to numb the suffering. It is their way of dealing with the pain. What these addicts needed more than anything else is love, compassion and understanding. And that was the purpose of the drug centre that I set up.

The aim of the centre was to help addicts to come off drugs and to show them that there is always a way out of addiction. The object of the therapy was to help them see the light at the end of the tunnel. They come to accept they too can be loved. And they accept that they are as good as anyone else and come to find peace within themselves. The persistent use of drugs leads the users to have strong suicidal tendencies. When they get help these tendencies abate and they find new and better ways of coping.

Addiction can also be inherited genetically through the family line. Prayer can help to break the chain. Children are often influenced by being brought up in an atmosphere where people regularly drink and take drugs. Young people begin to see this as a normal pattern of behaviour.

Judging is not what addicts need. What they need is help. They need someone to show them how to overcome their problems in a different way and give them the ability to overcome their addiction. The centre is also used to rehabilitate teen alcoholics and all kinds of substance abuse.

The centre has to date helped a lot of young people. The Minister for Health in Ireland formally opened it as an official unit. Many young people have given testimonies as to how they were aided to overcome their drug and alcohol abuse; how they were given a second chance at education and how they began to see that life was worth living again. Some of the youth had come to the spot in a state where they felt they were at the end of the road and had no control in lives that were ruled by their passion to get one more fix. Thank God that young lives have been turned around.

Centre to treat troubled boys

IRELAND'S first ever residential treatment centre for teenage boys with alcohol and drug abuse problems opened its doors this week.

The Matt Talbot Adolescent Services, which has been operating day care programmes in two locations in Cork city, helps teenagers who are substance abusers.

Having treated teenage boys on a day–care basis, staff felt that a full–time residential centre was needed to cater for the young people.

The new centre, which is in Ahiohill, near Clonakilty in west Cork, will cater for six boys aged between 14 and 19 years.

Ann Ruxton, a family support worker at the centre, said: "We have been fighting for this for the last five years and are delighted that the centre is finally opened."

She added: "The centre is unique in that it not only cares for the boys' needs, but we also concentrate on their families. While there are many centres

By DEIRDRE O'REILLY
deirdre.oreilly@eecho.ie

in the country that cater for teenage substance abusers, ours is the only centre that takes all the family into consideration.

"While the boys are with us, their whole lives will be turned around to prepare them to go back home and it if saves just one life, it will be worth it.

"But this is just the tip of the iceberg. We have only six beds in the centre and our needs are so much bigger than that. We are now hoping to open another centre in the near future."

Funding for the unique centre has been granted through the departments of justice and education, the Southern Health Board and the VEC.

Each of the boys will stay at the west Cork centre for between three and six months.

During that time, they will be treated for their addiction and will also receive training, education and spiritual and emotional guidance.

From The Irish Examiner

Minister pledges teen rehab centres

by Mary Dundon
Political Reporter

HEALTH Minister Micheál Martin has promised to fund residential drug and alcohol treatment centres for teenagers nationwide, if a €800,000 pilot project he opened yesterday succeeds.

The minister was responding to criticism of the State for failing to deliver proper residential care for teenage drug and alcohol abusers.

Following the official opening of the first holistic drug and alcohol treatment centre for teenagers in the country, Mr Martin said: "We will carry out an assessment of need for these centres nationwide and, if this one is successful, we will use it as a model for other treatment centres around the country."

The Matt Talbot Residential Treatment Centre for Adolescents, opened in West Cork yesterday, finally got State funding after a seven-year campaign. Family support worker Ann Ruxton said there is a huge need for other centres like the one near Bandon, which will cater for seven adolescents:

Micheál Martin: responds to criticism over care.

"The resources given to this problem so far have only touched the tip of the iceberg and we need major State funding for other centres."

Matt Talbot director of services Geraldine Ring said: "The State needs to provide holistic treatment centres like ours in every Health Board region."

Mr Martin said that most young people can deal with their drug problem as outpatients with parents and family supporting them and the State funds outpatient programmes in every Health Board district. The National Drugs Strategy has given a commitment to provide a residential treatment programme for under-18s while a group set up by the Minister will report shortly on specific action to be taken.

From The Irish Examiner

Drug care centre for Bandon

A €1 million plus residential centre for male teenage addicts is to open in County Cork.

Minister for Health and Children Micheál Martin TD has cleared the way for the Matt Talbot Adolescent Services to open the centre at Ahiohill House in Bandon. Plans to open the facility were temporarily scuppered last September when the board of the Matt Talbot Adolescent Services resigned due to a disagreement with the Southern Health Board about a treatment model. But following discussions between the groups the board returned, a resolution was reached and the project was put back on track.

The new centre — the second of its kind in Ireland — is scheduled to open in September. It will cater for between six to eight male adolescents aged between 14 and 18 years old. They will be able to stay at the house for up to six months at a time.

From
The Evening Echo

PRAYER OF AN ALCOHOLIC

My hands are chained; my feet are tied,
All my tears I have drunk and dried.
I cannot walk, there`s no path to follow,
I am behind bars. I cannot reap or sow.
I have an addiction; I'm an alcoholic,
My life is in danger, living is chronic.
Loosen my feet, Lord, I want to walk,
And in my prayers to You I want to talk.
Free my hands for good, instead of drinking,
Help me keep afloat instead of sinking,
Help me to follow every step I need to take,
To never give up, to light a fire in the lake.
I need You here, Lord, I need You now,
Teach me, because I do not know how.
Give me a life in You which I have never known
And help me to trust in Your strength to keep me going.
Let my past life be the guidance to my future;
Lord, I ask You today and forever, to be my tutor.

Living in Him Forever

In 1990 a lady called to my door in great pain. She said she was contemplating suicide, as her daughter was pregnant after being raped. Her sons were on drugs and they were stealing to feed their habits. Her husband was in hospital with his nerves. I had never been to a prayer meeting and knew nothing about the healing ministry, but I felt so sorry for her. I sat some distance away from her and I started to pray and to my amazement I started to cry and cry and I did not know why. All of a sudden she said she felt great peace and all her thoughts of suicide were gone.

Shortly after that, this lady sent people to me who were depressed. When I prayed with them I cried out their pain. Then a friend called with cancer of the breast which was at an advanced stage. She had no religion but I told her to believe in the power of God and to trust in him and to believe that God could do anything. I then prayed with her and she had a great healing. All the pain left instantly. I then knew that God was using me as a channel to heal people.

There are different kinds of healing. Inner healing is the healing of memories for all who have suffered and who need healing from their past and forgiveness for all the bitterness and resentment they have held on to. There is spiritual healing of those that have walked away from God to follow other gods, such as money, pleasure, drugs, pornographic videos and new age practices. Physical healing is the healing of all our illnesses, and any sickness that besets us. Psychological healing is the healing of mental illness and emotional problems. All our compulsions are ingrained ways of thinking and speaking. Jesus wants to heal the whole person because Jesus has been resurrected (Jesus is the same yesterday, today and forever). Jesus came on earth to set us free and he came so that all might be saved. Jesus wants us all to be with him in heaven as he said in John 14 verse 2, " In my father's house there are many mansions if it was not so I would have told you I go to prepare a place for you". No matter what religion we practice or what our race or colour, with Jesus we are all one family and all his children. God is our Father, and Mary our Queen and our mother.

Once a priest was put in my way and he told me that he had lost his faith. He said that he found it impossible to pray and was contemplating leaving the priesthood. He was a curate in a parish in England. I prayed with him and I told him he suffered from depression. I told him not to pray in words but just to sit in silences in the church and ask Jesus to heal him with His healing love. I advised him not to leave the priesthood and when I met him some time later he was on top of the world and very happy in the priesthood. I still keep in contact with him and we are great friends.

Shortly after that I went to a charismatic prayer meeting and instantly got the gift of tongues. This is another way of praying to God in the Spirit. When the apostles were assembled in the upper room in Pentecost the Holy Spirit came upon them in forms of tongues of fire and they all started singing and praising God in different tongues (languages). When you yield to the Holy Spirit, the Spirit of God takes over. God gave me the gift of wisdom and knowledge. I know instantly when people are in to witchcraft and new age practices such as Reiki healing, hypnotism, ke massage, yoga, reflexology, and fortune telling and reading horoscopes.

I was at a prayer meeting once in Boston and afterwards I was asked to pray with people. A lady from Africa put her hand on my shoulder and immediately I could feel evil; no matter how I tried I could not pray. Then I said a short prayer over this lady and she left. Afterwards, when she left, it was revealed to me that she was into witchcraft and other pagan practices that they do in Africa. When I pray with people who are into occult practices they are released. Deliverance is a release from evil spiritual influences, which oppress a person or hinder the individual response to God's saving grace. Some holy people that are in prayer may also need release if they are carrying evil from their ancestors, ancestral guilt, bondage and ancestral curses. To curse a person or to wish them evil in any way is very wrong but all curses can be lifted through prayer. We should always wish people well and forgive people who hurt us; as Jesus said, " Forgive and you will be forgiven", " Judge not and you will not be judged".

Then, shortly after that, God gave me a stronger gift of visions. He revealed to me in a vision, events of my future life and different places where He wanted me to visit. He showed me events in the bible and I also see a lot of the Holy souls in need of prayer. When young girls come to visit me I instantly know if any of them has had a miscarriage or an abortion, as I can see the baby not as a foetus but as a beautiful baby or a small child. If anyone has lost a child in a cot death or any other way Jesus shows me the baby and it gives great comfort to the parents. I went to Medjugorje with Brian when he was very ill and had some wonderful experiences there. I saw all kinds of visions; in the room I slept in, the church and the mountains. I even had a vision one night of the end of the world.

We should always monitor the viewing of television for our children. One evening I was praying for a young couple who had difficulty in controlling their children and said that their children were always angry and never seemed to be happy with one another. Jesus told me that the television should be thrown out of their house. One night recently I had a vision when I saw a television with the screen full of flames of fire, and I could see people walking through the flames. I then saw a vision of Jesus scourged and crowned with thorns on His own in the screen. A great sadness came over me and I felt as if we were scourging Jesus again with the evil we were allowing our children to watch.

I have seen hundreds of different saints in visions as well as scenes of God's beautiful creation and lots of different trees. I also see dark shadows walking through the trees that show the evil one trying to destroy God's creation.

I pray for the unborn because a lot of young girls do not realise the evil of abortion and that it is another form of murder. A lovely young girl visited me recently and she said quite innocently that she had terminated her pregnancy because the doctor had advised her to, owing to some abnormality. She asked me to pray for her that God would bless her with another baby. Recently God gave me a beautiful gift of baby tongues and I use it when I am praying for sick babies.

Then some people called to see me who were involved in the occult and wanted deliverance from evil spirits. When I began to pray with them they were released and I knew that Jesus was using me to help other people through this gift. Then some people came to me who had been traumatised and God in His mercy gave me the gift of counselling the broken hearted.

PRAYER OF PROTECTION, HEALING AND RELEASE

Put on God's armour to resist the devil's antics (Eph 6) and do not interfere with the Lord's work in your life; put on shields of faith to put out the arrows of the evil one; accept the salvation of God as your helmet and receive his word as your sword. Heavenly Father, please show me the way and explain any way that Satan has a hold on my life. I let go of any territory I have handed over to Satan and reclaim it under the Lordship of Jesus Christ. In the name of Jesus I bind all spirits of the air, ground, underground and the nether world. I bind all forces of evil and claim the blood of Jesus Christ in the air, atmosphere, the water, the ground and their fruits around the underground, the nether world and me. In the name of Jesus Christ I seal this room and all members of my family and relatives in the blood of Jesus Christ. In the name of Jesus Christ I forbid every spirit from any source from harming me in any way. In the name of Jesus Christ I regret the seductive lure of evil in all its form and to let sin have no domination over me. I reject Satan and all His empty promises.

Heavenly father, I ask forgiveness for myself, friends and relatives and ancestors for falling upon powers that set them up in opposition against you. Forgive them Lord, for they did not know what they were doing. Jesus, I renounce all openness to the cult of false worships and benefits of magical arts. I renounce every power apart from God and every part of worship that does not honour you, Jesus Christ. I renounce fortune telling, Tarot cards and occult games. I break the curses that may be coming against me and my family and stop the transmission of these curses coming from my ancestors. I bind you away from me in Jesus' name. Lord Jesus, fill me with your love to replace the fear. Fill me with your strength to replace the weakness. Lord Jesus, fill me with your health and take away any illness that affects me. Loving Lord let the cleansing water of my baptism flow back through the generation of my family and through the lines of contamination, to purify my family. This prayer will release you from your past and heal you.
Amen

THE PRISON WALLS ARE MELTED DOWN

One day a young girl came to my door to help me with Brian. She was a lovely, friendly girl and she poured out her life story to me. It was a horror story; she had a childhood of hell. I was so taken aback that I asked her if she would like me to pray with her. When I was praying with her she was touched powerfully by the Holy Spirit and instantly got all the gifts of the Holy Spirit. I took her under my wing, as she had no mother while growing up. We are now very close and she is like an extra daughter to me.

OUR LOVE TOGETHER

1990 Brian and myself started to pray the rosary and many other prayers together and he knew his prayers almost to the very end. We worked together in the garden as I always loved gardening and I made a beautiful rose garden. I knew my garden was special as I got a heavenly perfume from the Holy Spirit in it. I got the same peace there as I would have in a church. I told my friends that it was like a church without a roof, and that I thought of putting up a grotto to our Lady as I had always had a great devotion to her since I had the vision when I was 12 years old. I also thought of putting in the Stations of the Cross. Brian and myself used to love going for walks around the garden.

A Journey that lasts a Lifetime

In the mid-1990s the Holy Father revealed to Mary that my whole life was going to change. My rose garden was going to become a garden of prayer and the name of the garden was going to be 'A Moment with Jesus and Mary`. Mary is blessed with a powerful gift of prophecy; she gets prophetic messages, prayers and holy songs from the Holy Spirit and she told me that I was going to have 2 holy wells, one in honour of the Little child of Innocence and one in honour of St Margaret. Mary was very excited and overjoyed at this wonderful news and said that my house was going to become a house of prayer.

The colours and the design of each room in the house and garden were revealed. As blue and pink are Our Lady`s colours, they are the main colours used in the house and the garden and every room in the house has been changed to these colours. We have three chapels in the garden, one in honour of Little Nellie, one for bible reading and confession and the third is used for healing.

As you can see from the photographs the garden is completed. It took two years of hard work as we ran into a lot of difficulties. At one stage I became so stressed out because I could not get anyone to complete the work of the wells. This was very unnecessary stress, as everything that is planned by God is completed by Him.

The garden was opened in August 2001 with mass and prayers and a special blessing. A lot of people attended the opening day and it was a great success. There are a lot of Prayers and chaplets that are said in the garden and a lot of healing is received through these. The garden is open from April to October with special prayers from three to four every day. We have prayer meetings, night vigils and mass every month.

Already miracles have happened and everyone who enters the garden gets great healing, some get the gifts of the Holy Spirit and some the gift of Faith. Just recently, a chronic heroin addict arrived from Dublin and when he drank water from the well he could feel a sensation going right through him and had a great healing. When I prayed with his son he was powerfully healed emotionally as he had suffered all his life through watching his father with the after effects of heroin.

Some people are healed from their depression and all leave the garden with a great heavenly peace. Mary, Martina and myself work as a team in the healing ministry, in the garden and the house.

THY WILL BE DONE ON EARTH

In 1992 God gave me a ministry with travellers. It was revealed to me that I was to visit all the halting sites up and down the country. They are a big part of my life as I also have a phone ministry with them and they are now like an extended family to me. They visit my garden in large numbers and receive great healing. They have contributed so generously with statues and donations for the garden.

One day a young man by the name of Frank entered my garden in a wheelchair; he was very ill and he died soon afterwards but he was a very holy man and he gave me a lovely crucifix for the garden. The night he died he came to me for prayer and it was revealed to me that he was to spend 4 weeks in purgatory. I got masses said for him and I prayed for him and he went to heaven in a short while. Frank told me I was to be the mother of all travellers and his words have come true, because I try to guide them and direct them like a mother does.

In the year 2000 it was revealed that I was to travel to all prayer meetings up and down the country, giving my testimony about how God had healed me of my broken childhood. I have also travelled to England and Scotland and America and I plan in the future to travel around Europe.

TESTIMONIES

Testimony of Lisa Sabrina Maughan

Little Lisa Sabrina called to my garden on June 2002. She had travelled from Bradford in England with her parents Sean and Winifred and her mother was very upset as little Lisa suffered from a hole in the heart and also a kidney and liver complaint. When she went back to her doctor in England to discuss surgery, he took a scan and told her that her heart was perfect. He could find no explanation so he did a further scan and this was completely clear and he told her to call in a year's time for a check up. Lisa Sabrina called back to me in October 2002 and she is a perfect little baby.

Testimony of Michael Wallace (Cork City)

Michael had a powerful physical and spiritual healing in God's Holy Garden, 'A Moment with Jesus & Mary'. When God heals he heals the total person because we are made up of body, soul and spirit. Michael was a chronic alcoholic and, as a result of his drinking, he developed sclerosis of the liver. He had a suspected tumour on the liver, seven and a half inches long, and he also suffered from severe stress, depression and anxiety. Michael visited me nine to ten times in all before he was completely healed. During this period Michael was in and out of hospital several times. God healed him in stages to test his faith.

After his first visit here Michael went back to his doctor; the doctor did an ultra sound and said that it was remarkable that the tumour had reduced to two inches. He had two biopsies and when he had the second biopsy the doctor told him the tumour was gone. Michael visited his doctor in August 2002 who gave him the all clear and said he can visit him later for a check- up. Michael is not on any treatment and he says he has never felt better. All stress, anxiety and depression have gone from him and the longing for drink has also disappeared. He is now in deep prayer and his faith is very strong; he now trusts in the divine physician for all his problems. Every time he visits the garden he receives peace and he said he had a vision one night after leaving here. He is now back working full time.

Testimony of Michael Junior Wallace(Mayfield Cork City)

Michael called here about five years ago with his parents. Michael was suffering from severe headaches. When I prayed with him, God revealed to me that his headaches were the result of an accident and Michael then told me he had had an accident on his bicycle. As I prayed with him he rested in the Holy Spirit and he was deeply touched by Jesus. He was healed instantly of his headaches and has never had a headache since. Michael completed his time in school and is now working full time.

Testimony of Christina Mc Donnagh

Christina travelled here from Wales with a very severe back problem and was unable to walk. When I prayed with her on the telephone she had a partial healing from Jesus and then she decided to visit my garden. Jesus gave her a healing in the garden. She now walks perfectly and even had a baby this year. Christina has been very generous to me and her way of thanking Jesus is she has donated statues and pictures for my garden and my chapels.

Testimony of a local women

A lot of local people come as well to my garden to pray and they all say they find peace. A local woman named Nicola called to my home one day in great pain. She had advanced cancer and said that she had no religion but did believe in God. I asked her if she believed that God could do anything and I said to her that nothing was impossible to God, that all she needed was faith and trust. I prayed with her and God cured her immediately. She is now enjoying great health.

I also visit nursing homes and prisons. Hospitals and prisons are lonely places so it is very important that the prisoners' relations visit them.

I get letters from people all over Ireland and England looking for prayers and advice. I got a very sad letter, one day, from a lady that lived in England. Her husband, who was a chronic drug addict, had been recently released from prison. He got involved with a teenage girl, whose family were drug abusers. This wife never lost hope and prayed all the time to God and our Lady; she stuck by her husband through thick and thin. When he requested a divorce she refused and told him that she loved him, as well as his children. She won him back through love and prayer. Love conquers all. Her story is an example to other couples that are in the same situation. You must never give up hope and you must allow God to work in your marriage because what God joins together no man can put asunder. People nowadays forget that marriage is for life and that they must stay together in good times and bad.

Prayers Received from Jesus

Strength Prayer

Lord Jesus, I hand over to you my sufferings, my joys and my sorrows of this day and I ask you take care of them so I will not be led astray.

Each day Lord may I start afresh with you and carry out your will. Make my weaknesses stronger to worship you O, my Lord, My God. Jesus, may I follow you each day and live a life of prayer.

Amen

Sweet Angel

I come before you as a little child, give me strength in mind, body and soul. Keep me pure and chaste and never let me cut my friends heart out with gossip.

Give me the heart of a little child that never sins or disobeys your words. It's by praying and keeping the commandments, you, Lord, set me free and give me a life eternally. Praise the Lord, the finder and the redeemer.

Amen.

Salvation

Lord Jesus, we press our wounds close to your heart so we can be healed. The body and blood you gave us Lord Jesus is our feast for salvation.

As you were crucified on the cross, Lord Jesus, we plead with you to allow the blood of your temple that was pierced, to dip down unto us so we can have a new life with you.

We pray Lord that your will and ours will be one. Through your sacred wounds, Lord, we can become one with you. Give us the healing power Lord, to bring your healing words to others.

I now believe, Lord, that I am healed through your wounds, I place my life in your hands. I ask you to forgive my sins of the past and be with me for the rest of my life, so I will not sin against you. Through your love Jesus I am purified and I live for you, with you and for all eternity,

Amen.

Our love together

When I arrived in Bandon in 1990, I settled in at once into my new home. I prayed a lot of rosaries, with Brian, as he knew his prayers almost to the end of his life. I also prayed rosaries with people who called. Praying gave me great peace and strength to carry on.

One day as I was hanging the clothes, out on the line, the most beautiful smell of perfume wafted up to me. It was no ordinary perfume, and it was followed by a deep peace. I got the same peace as you would get in a church. I invited some of my friends into my garden, to see if they could experience the same peace in case it was my imagination. They experienced the same peace. I realised my garden was like a church without a roof.

Then I started a prayer meeting in my house. One night during the prayer meeting, a man got a prophetic message. He said: "Your garden is no ordinary garden. A priest was murdered in the upper corner of the garden during the troubled times in Ireland." He added that this priest had been in France, but was advised not to return to Bandon. All this occurred in Ireland at a time when priests were on the run. The neighbourhood where I live was known as "Gallows Hill" and the wall of my garden was reputed to be the place where they hung Catholics during a period of religious discrimination.

Brian loved to walk around the garden, which was a walled in garden. It was very safe for him. I thought of putting a grotto in the centre of the garden, and Stations of the Cross on the wall. I had a lovely rose garden and I was always interested in gardening. I took great pride in my garden. The flowers to me were like the flowers blooming in Heaven, with so many colours and varieties.

One day, I wanted to go to the shop to get milk, and on this occasion Brian refused to come with me. A young girl, named Mary came to my rescue. She stayed with Brian until I came back. We started chatting and she gradually began to open her heart to me, and tell me the story of her life. It was no ordinary story. It was a horror story. Her childhood was a hell on earth. I was shocked when I heard her story. I asked her if she would like me to pray with her. As I was praying with her, the Holy Spirit touched her powerfully. She instantly received all the gifts of the Holy Spirit. I took her under my wing, as she had no mother growing up. We are now very close, and we are great friends ever since.

In the mid 1990s Mary and myself had built up a good relationship. She came from such a broken home; I spent a lot of time praying with her. One day as we were praying the rosary together. God gave her a powerful message, about how my garden was going to be transformed. It was going to be changed into a Prayer Garden. She also got a message that my house was going to become a house of prayer.

I immediately started to change the house around. The colours and the design of each room in the house were revealed to me in prayer. Blue and pink are Our lady's colours, and they are the main colours used in the house and garden. Every room in the house was changed to these colours. I also put altars in honour of Our lady and the Sacred heart of Jesus in different places. One of my upstairs rooms was converted into a prayer room, where people could come and pray.

I was very excited, and overjoyed at this wonderful news. I asked this question: "Why has God chosen me, my house and my garden?" I was a bit apprehensive because I was told in prayer that, the work in the garden was going to be difficult. I did not realise that it was going to be so difficult. At every stage I encountered stress, but this was unnecessary because if God is for us who can be against us as it says in scripture.

First I dug up my roses, and made a path around the garden. I felt that I was guided stage by stage by the Holy Spirit. I put a solid foundation in the centre, for a Lourdes grotto. A rosary chain was made of stones around the grotto. I made it with my grandchildren. The name of the garden is 'A Moment with Jesus and Mary'

I have three wells in the garden; one in honour of the little child of Innocence, and one in honour of Saint Margaret Mary. The third one is a fountain-well, dedicated to Saint John the Baptist,. in memory of the baptism of Jesus. The wells were hand dug and it was very hard work as the garden is made of rocky ground.

The next stage comprised of three chapels one of which was dedicated to Little Nellie of Holy God. She was a child-saint from Cork. I pray in this chapel, for sick babies and sick children. The second chapel is dedicated to bible reading. When people are finished praying in the garden, they read the bible in this chapel, and say their own private prayers. The third chapel is called the healing chapel; I use this chapel for praying with people for healing. Pilgrims also pray in it, for their own intentions. This chapel is also used for confessions when Mass is said in the garden.

The next stage was putting up the Stations of the Cross, and the mysteries of the rosary. As it is a walled in garden, about forty-foot high, we had plenty of wall-space. We put large pictures, and various statues of saints. A large statue of the Sacred heart was put in the left hand corner. A large statue of Our Lady was put in the right hand corner. In between these two statues, an altar was built, where Mass is said during the summer months.

This year seven alcoves were erected on the left-hand side of the garden. The whole garden is now covered with concrete slabs. At first I missed my green grass, but as time went on, I realised it saved me a lot of work.

As you can see from the photographs, the garden is now completed. It took four years-of hard work, and I ran into a lot of difficulties, but with the help of God and Our Lady everything was accomplished.

The garden was opened in August 2001 with Mass and prayers and a special Blessing . A lot of people attended the opening day and it was a great success . There are a lot of prayers and chaplets said in the garden and a lot of healing is received through these prayers. The garden is open from April to October with special prayers from three to four every day We have prayer meetings, night vigils and Mass every month.

Already miracles have happened and everyone who enters the garden gets great healing - some get the gifts of the Holy Spirit and some the gift of Faith. Just recently, a chronic heroin addict arrived from Dublin and when he drank the holy water from the well he could feel a sensation going right through him and he received a great healing . When I prayed with his son he was powerfully healed emotionally as had suffered all his life, watching his father with the after affects of heroin.

Some people are healed from their depression and all claim they experience a great heavenly peace in the holy garden.

ME AND YOU

Me and you and you and me
What a beautiful love between us you see
Happy together we can feel free
How precious our lives must be
You and me and me and you,

What a great combination.
By our wonderful ,God the mason,
In our lives He give us graces,
He asked for us to be together He never forces,
What is yours is mine and what is mine is yours,
Together God has given us our cures,
We are like birds of a feather that flap together
Like gloves that have a perfect fit

Testimonies

Testimony of Michael McDonagh

Michael was a young boy with Muscular dystrophy. He travelled here from London two years ago with his mother and received a partial healing. Then Michael called six months ago, as he had developed a blood disorder. He went back to his doctor three days later and the doctor said he was completely cured. Praise the name of Jesus.

Testimony of Geraldine Heaphy

Geraldine called to my garden a year ago complaining of cancer. She had a large tumour in her oesophagus and the doctor told her to eat well, as after her operation she would be unable to eat for a long time. She called here, to the garden, every Sunday for nine weeks as a novena and had a full course of chemotherapy and radium treatment. When she went for a scan, to the amazement of the doctors the tumour had disappeared. She called here a few weeks back to pray in thanksgiving in the holy garden. She said she had never felt better and enjoyed such health.

Testimony of Patrick McDonagh

Patrick rang me from England in great distress. He said his lower lip was very painful and sore and when he went to the doctor he was diagnosed as having a bad infection and was put on a lot of courses of antibiotics. He then visited my garden and when I prayed with him I knew he had cancer. He went back to England and the doctor told him he had cancer. During his treatment his tongue, lip and jaw were burned but when he came back again to visit my garden God cured him. All the soreness went and even the red colour left him. He is now in perfect health and has the 'all clear' from the cancer.

Testimony of Rose an elderly lady

Rose suffered a lot of pain in her shoulder and her grand-child gave her holy water from the garden. She put some of the holy water on her shoulder every night for some weeks and her shoulder is now cured and she no longer complains of pain.

Testimony of Sean and Mairead

When Mairead visited my garden she was very distressed, as Sean had walked out on her five years previously leaving her with four children to rear. I prayed that God would work a miracle and bring them back together because what God has joined together no man should separate. Three months ago he walked back into her life and thank God and Our Lady that they are now very happy together. Nothing is impossible to God, all we have to do is trust in His love and mercy and never give up hope. Perseverance in prayer is very important.

Testimony of Michael Coffee from Kerry

Michael called here to the garden six months ago. Michael has Tuberculosis, was taking twelve tablets daily and was to have an operation on his lung. From the scan you can see the damage. He called here nine times as a novena, then went back to Crumlin hospital in Dublin two months ago and the doctor said he had im-proved so much that no surgery was needed. He is now taking only six tablets a day. When he has to go back to the hospital again I am hoping that God, in His Divine mercy and love, will completely cure him. Michael is a twelve-year-old boy.

Testimony of four young boys (Stephan, Jimmy, Patrick and Darren)

Four boys who are all cousins suffered from their feet when they arrived in my garden last year. It was a genetic complaint and apparently the skin on their feet used to get very sore and bleed on occasions. They could only wear soft runners and two pairs of socks and even at that their feet were painful. I washed their feet at a special Shrine in my garden and when they came back two weeks later they said their feet had not bled since they had been in the garden. They are now wearing leather shoes and their feet are no longer sore. All power, honour and glory to Jesus.

Testimony of Patrick Hallissey

Patrick came to my garden two years ago suffering from depression. He had been in a psychiatric hospital for a period after being bullied in school and his mother had taken him to various new age healers. He had to come here several times but thank God he is now enjoying great health. His mother is a wonderful person, but she did not realise that involvement in new age is wrong and it slowed down his healing.

Testimony of Fourteen People healed of depression

On the 24th of Aug 2003 we had a day of prayer in the garden. A large crowd attended and we had mass, healing prayers etc. It was the 100th anniversary of Little Nellie. Fourteen people claimed to have been healed. I feel myself healing in the garden of my broken childhood when I pray with people.

A lot of broken marriages have been restored, a lot of drug addicts and alcoholics have given up their bad habits, broken relationships have been healed and people who have not spoken to one another in years make friends again in the garden.

Testimony of a young child from England

A young child from England called recently who had dislocated hips and a back complaint. Since I prayed with him he has been completely cured. He only came here once and was healed. God heals in different ways.

Those are some of the testimonies of healings in my holy garden. All power, honour and glory to God who is overflowing with streams of love, mercy and compassion. In Him we have our hope, our joy and our salvation.

THE ROSE BUSH

When you think of a rose bush, think how beautiful it looks. The colours of the flowers are radiant with light and the smell of their perfume would put your heart on fire. What a beautiful invention by the Lord! When I look at the rose bush, I can never understand why such beautiful flowers stand on prickly thorns. When you pick a rose in your hands, thorns prick you. The same applies when you are coming to God. You fight your way along the paths in your life that are evil, and get rid of all the thorns in your way.

When you have achieved all, what a beautiful token you will receive. When Jesus was crucified, the thorns were his sufferings, and the rose His resurrection.

When I was a child, my life started as a thorn bush, then on top of the briar grew a rose. A rose resembles victory, in every walk of life. Where God is, the devil will try to stand, but God will always be ahead of him, standing on top of him, so you can understand the story of the rose.

THE DOOR WHERE HIS MERCY FLOWS

As you come in please say a prayer,
So Jesus can heal you within layer by layer,
He is ready to listen to all your pains and aches,
He is the loving Lord, who gives and not takes,
His love overflows and can change your heart,
So now as you pray you can make a new start.
This door you enter will bring forth light,
Never again will you be in the dark but the bright,
Bring in your family bring in your friends,
So they too can be forgiven and make amends.
Talk to God and pray with great dedication,
And His wonderful power will heal the nation.

THE LITTLE CHILD OF INNOCENCE

The Little child of innocence is very much part of my garden. I have a large picture of her hanging in my holy garden on the wall also one of the healing wells is dedicated to her. Little Sandra is a gift from God to help little children. She was born on the 19th of April 1985. She was a very happy baby normal in every way.

Her life dramatically changed when she was 2 years old she became very ill. Neuroblastoma cancer was diagnosed. The doctors removed the tumour and little Sandra had to go for chemotherapy treatment. She had no ill effects apart from hair loss. She was a very bright intelligent little girl who suffered a lot of pain.

In spite of her own suffering she would run to comfort other children who were in pain in the hospital. She had a special love for lonely abandoned children and she showed these children great love. She loved music and had a great gift of joy. She was always in great humour and tried to hide her pain.

When she got secondories with the cancer, she refused self- pity and was heroic in her suffering. In the final weeks she never complained although her pain was intense.

She died on Christmas day at the age of 3 years, while her parents were at mass, receiving Holy Communion. She died at 12 noon at that moment a rainbow was seen in the sky. Little Sandra never sinned, as she died not come to the use of reason. She entered heaven by the means of her baptism. So you see how important it is to have children baptised. Baptism is the gate to the sacraments necessary for salvation. Baptism is the sacrament that welcomes us into the family of God. Unless a man is born of water and the spirit he cannot enter into the kingdom of God.

When we get baptised we put on Christ, it is like a bath that purifies us. We are born with a fallen human nature tainted by original sin. So we need a new baptism to be freed from the power of darkness and brought into the realm of the freedom of the family of God. Baptism is a sacrament of faith, but for the grace to unfold the parents help is very important. Each year the church celebrates at the Easter Vigil the renewal of baptismal promises.

Sandra seemed guided by grace to live a holy life. God is working through her in heaven, like he guided her on earth

" Unless you become like little children you cannot enter into the kingdom of God" She has answered all kinds of requests, selling homes, obtaining jobs, healing of cancer and helping people cope with sick children.

The Little Child Of Innocence plays a very important role in my garden. I have a large picture of her where people can pray through her intercession. I have one of the healing wells in the garden dedicated in her honour. This is the chaplet we say walking around the well for healing.

HEALING CHAPLET TO LITTLE SANDRA

1 Our Father
1 Hail Mary
1 Glory Be
Say the above 3 times
Little Child Of Innocence Pray for us (3 times)

POEM ABOUT THE
CHILD OF INNOCENCE'S

You were a child so meek and mild,
Even though your life was only for a while,
You gave the world such beauty,
Jesus has given you His fruit,
You did not have to say a word just been mute
Jesus loves you the way you are,
You were His shining little star,
Your wisdom was not by years,
As a child you had no fears,
Your short life was taken,
Because he wanted you from His creation,
To help the world from all its affliction,
He knew with His help it would be purification.

MY GARDEN OF PRAYER
(A MOMENT WITH JESUS AND MARY)

My Holy garden is in the image and likeness of God. What inspiration He gave me, I followed. Many people enter my garden that are heavily burdened but when they go out of the gate they have a different attitude, even if their problems are not solved. Attitude is more important than facts. It is as if they get a grip on their lives and say, 'I can go through with it, I will be strong'. They receive hope, which is a powerful gift, and they use this hope to heal themselves. God gives them wisdom and knowledge, and fills them with peace. This sets them straight; it is God's will within them that pushes them to strive. I remind them, that every time they say, ' I can't`, to say, the word, ' I can`. The more they use this phase, the more powerful it becomes in their mind and it takes over the negative thinking, even if they never receive any physical or emotional healing. This alone will be the greatest healing that they could ever have, to be able to take control of their own lives.

People who have been traumatised, or who need physical or emotional healing are those who come in large numbers. They come because they are desperate. They have gone down all roads to try and solve their problems and they finally realise that they cannot rely on their own strength or abilities, and that they need a Higher Power.

A lot of people have told me that they were inspired to come and visit my garden and they go out of the door happy. They all say that they get tremendous peace and joy in this holy garden. it is a place of pilgrimage where people come and absorb the peace.

I see people mainly by appointment on weekdays. The garden is open from April to October and on Sunday it is opened all year round. I am very committed to my work in the garden, because it is God's work. I look on it as my vocation. I enjoy doing it and I pray that God's will be done in people's lives.

People do not realise how powerful prayer is. If we pray for those who need prayer, we can save their lives. I do not just pray with people and say this is the end. I pray for them, at my prayer meeting, and my prayer time during the day, so they are never forgotten. Everyone is welcome, all classes of society, all cultures, and all religions. I am a servant of God, to His people, providing the word of truth. It can change people's lives if they trust in Jesus.

As time goes by, the garden is becoming better known. It is the first of its kind in Ireland, and, knowing Irish people, including myself, I know they do not like change. This is a new era of faith, when new things are happening. This garden marks an era of changing times. God is love and He presents himself in many ways, in people's hearts.

It all started in the Garden of Eden. A garden of prayer goes back a long way, to the time of creation. In my garden, much fruit is ripened in people's lives. They have come back and told me. I am so happy that life has changed for them.

A HEALING CHILD'S STORY

My name is Mary. I am now going to give you my testimony about how I was healed by Jesus. For the first fifteen years of my life I lived with my Father. I lived in a trailer up to the age of eight years. For the first few years of my life things in my family were bad. I was always left on my own as a child. My Father used to beat me and as a result of the beatings and the stress he caused me I developed seizures and I used to get a lot of them over the years. I always had to go to hospital for periods of my childhood.

We had no running water in the caravan and we had no electricity. We used candles for light and my Father dug a well in the ground for us to have drinking water. I often used to see rats swimming in the well but this was still the water we drank. When I was eight we got a house and the conditions were better for a short time. Then he started to burn the carpets and the beds and I had to sleep on the floor. I had no food to eat, only stale bread that was often mouldy. It was the bread he used to get for the dogs. I was so hungry that sometimes I went into the farmer's field and pulled sugar beet.

Once I was old enough I went to school. I hated school because the teachers never liked me. I was a very destructive child and the teacher could not cope with me so she would pull me by the hair and drag me out into the cloakroom and push me behind the door. I was always mocked by the boys and was kicked and beaten till I was bruised.

I was very poorly dressed and wore dirty clothes. I was the talk of the school for the way I was dressed and the way I behaved. A new master came to the school when I went into third class. He hated me as well and joined in with the children in mocking me. He kicked me in the shins one day in front of everyone. I was so upset and my self-esteem was so low, I had no friends and nobody I could turn to.

The master said I was a very devious child. Because of the way life was for me at school and at home I was a slow learner and this was reflected in everything I did.

My Father started abusing me when I was a young child. He physically, sexually and mentally abused me and said the abuse was my entire fault. He abused me in every way possible until I was well into my teens. He left me with terrible fears; fears I thought I would never get over, but God in His love and mercy is healing me layer by layer.

My Father had tried to make me think like him in his evil ways, but thank God I never, ever thought like him and the evil things he did. My father had a mental illness and was in and out of mental hospitals quite a lot.

When I was a teenager I was taken from my Father and put in residential care to be looked after. Over a period of four years I was put into fourteen different homes where I suffered worse than at home. My bags were always packed and I was always on the move, I was bullied and looked down upon and noone wanted to know me because I had too many problems and noone could deal with my brokenness. I often thought of suicide and tried it on one occasion.

When I was living in one of the residential homes, one of the neighbours asked me to look after her husband who had Alzheimer's disease, while she went to the shop. This I did. When she returned I got chatting to her and told her all about my life and the abuse I suffered. This woman prayed with me and I instantly lay in the Spirit and received all the gifts of the Holy Spirit. My life started to get better because I knew God was healing me of my past. I got a new lease of life and started to feel happier in myself. This woman and I became like Daughter and Mother and got on so well.

I was so glad to meet my friend Eileen when I did, because she was a gift to me from God. She got me through everything. When I had lodging in my final year of school she was there for me and I used to go over to her house every evening. I completed my Leaving Cert. and got excellent results thanks to the hard effort I put in.

As bad as things were at home for me, all the moving around from home to home did me more damage. I firmly believe the worst home is better than the best institution, at least that was my experience. I never experienced love, or a feeling of belonging to any family. I never felt understood or listened to and felt betrayed in trust.

From school I went on to work with disadvantaged children. I worked here with girls my own age. I loved the children and I had so much love to give these children because I knew what it was like not to be loved or wanted. Life improved for me when I moved away from residential care and I knew that nobody could judge me because they would not know my story, nor where I lived. I do believe that I judged myself more than anyone else because I built up an inferiority complex about myself and believed everyone was against me. But God made me realise that there were beautiful people out there that would help me, without judging me, and soon I learned to stop condemning myself.

I realised I could not run away forever and that I had to face my fears, which I did, and it made me a stronger person with God's help. I now do not care what people think about me and if they judge me I realise that's their problem, not mine. We all are as good as we can be and that's the way I am. When God is for you nobody is against you.

I was proud of myself when I completed my course working with disadvantaged children because I feel I have achieved so much and I had noone to help me. I knew I did the right thing by doing the course. After finishing my course I came back home to work and rented my own apartment. I now have a very good job that I love. I learned to drive and now own my own car. I have also bought my own house.

As you can see, God can change peoples' lives around and out of the bad He can bring good. He can heal you if you allow Him to do so. I handed my whole life over to the Lord and asked Him that His will be done in me and not my will. He changed my life that day Eileen prayed over me and I take one day at a time now as Jesus taught me to.

Every time I pray to God to give me answers to my requests, sometimes He answers them differently from the way I expect, but He always answers my petitions. God will never put us in a situation that would be bad for us. We may get angry and say God does not answer our requests but, as we pray, God enlightens us about the problem and we realise He has the best answers. So, put your trust in Him today and say, 'Jesus, I trust in You'. He is the eternal Father and He knows best.

Prayers for healing

Healing of eye sight

Lord Jesus by the power of your Holy Spirit and the power of your Holy name reach out your hand and touch my eyes. Bathe them in your ocean of blood and water gushed forth for souls. I rebuke diseases of any kind in my eyes so I can see Lord, so I can see pictures of your glorious face, so I can see my family and friends and the beauty of the earth. Lord as well as giving me healing of my eyes give me spiritual sight so I can see the things you want me to see in people. Wash my eyes clean Lord and remove any infection from ever entering my eyes again. Just as a lady touched your cloak Lord who haemorrhaged for years. Give me an outstanding faith like her so I can put my faith in you for evermore so both my spiritual life and my life on earth will beam with your light and your glory.
Amen

Healing for people who are deaf

Lord Jesus I come before you and I ask for a miracle on my behalf. I would love to hear what people are saying and I would love to hear your word at mass so your word would come alive in me today. I pray fervently lord so you would come and put your healing hands on my ears so that the blood would circulate and I would hear and I would feel the warmth of your hands as you touched me. Cleanse my deafness from my ears with your precious blood and make my wounds heal.Unite my wounds to yours so I can live life to the maximum.

As I hear you Lord help me praise you, to glorify you and to honour you. Help me to believe today that even if you heal me in stages never to give up hope because I know Lord in your time I will be made whole again. I will make my prayer known

though the power of our Lord Jesus Christ. Save me my sufferings and help me to trust in your power and miracles.

Amen

Healing of faith

As I say a prayer to you today O' Lord help me to realise who
is God. Show me who is master before I carry on and create a
disaster. Teach me how to pray, listen and to obey. Show me the
directions and lead me the way. Help me to give up my sinful
ways before life makes me pay and I will be led to ruin and I
will end up with my self-inflicted wounds. You give me freedom
which can be fun but I know Lord unless I change I will lay on
my bed of chains. I will be in my prison cell and no one will
hear my bell, I'll be like the devil I will feel in hell.

Change me Lord before life changes me and because of it
I will have to flee. I won't repent because I feel you will not
forgive me so in your name I ask you to give me faith that will
never go out of date and that will teach me love and not hate
and remove my burdens and heavy weights off my shoulders. In
my heart their will be warmth and not the cold, meld me and
mould me and gently hold me and fold me in your love.

Bring your Holy Spirit upon me, wash me clean and make me
beam with your glorious light. Teach me your fatherly ways and
ask Our Lady to teach me her motherly ways throughout my life
of everyday. Give me peace, give me hope so I can follow you
as you guide the pope. O' gentle Jesus help me rise with you to
do your will, carry me over the hill. I believe today that I have a
profound faith and forever a Godly friendly mate.

Amen.

Healing of marriages

Heal my marriage gentle Lord make it last. What you join together no man can separate but my marriage is gone out the gate. Stop the fights and give me back my peace, If it is me Lord that needs changing come into my life turn my marriage around so we can love again. Pour your love into our hearts so that it will flow and not be of hate. Heal the depression and heal the wounds of my soul that down through the years I feel was stolen. Give me back my joy and give me back my hope so I do not have to struggle anymore. Teach me to cope. Remove my stubbornness and help me to tell the truth and not use my tongue to bad mouth about him.

Protect my children from such disaster give them hope and peace and love so that they do not judge just accept that something need change.

Jesus by the power and merits of your five most precious wounds take the thorns from my head that pierced you through. Heal me of all the anger, bitterness and the hatred I went through. Unite my sufferings with you Lord and make my thoughts and feelings whole again.

By the merits of your five most precious wounds heal the wounds of my left hand and my right hand for all the times I was punched and slapped and for all the times he beat me and caused bruises and broken bones in my hands. Heal me through and make me whole again.

Lord by the power of your five most precious wounds heal the wounds of my right and left leg that pierced you through in my legs each wound renew for my suffering, for my pain and my loss. As I feel I hang from a cross. Heal my broken legs, my broken toes and my bruises. Lord make me whole again.

By the merits of your five most precious wounds heal the wounds of my side from all the beatings I received, for all the days I suffered in bed and for all the torn muscles and horrific kicks into the stomach I could not eat. When my body did not function as a result heal me Lord and unite my sufferings to your five most precious wounds.

Heal the wounds of my soul and my body please Lord make me whole again. Live in my heart and if it is your will live in my husband's heart and give him a new start. Change his ways O' Lord make him be like you so that your beaming love and light will be shinning through. If it is your will Lord for us to be apart help our children and us to make a new start . Renew our friendships so that violence will no longer exist in our homes or in our hearts. Jesus as you were crucified save us anymore crosses in our marriage. Make us happy and travel along like a carriage.

Healing of sexual , mental and physical abuse

We are an island so tiny so small full perpetrators who were always on the call. Little children who lost everything they were put into orphanages run by nuns and priests and Christian brothers. Their little lives they were in a jails that were fenced they were beaten they were broken and abused. They did not know why they were always confused.

Their night time was a terror what was done to their friends was seen in a mirror. Their little lives so frail everything for them seemed to fail. Here today gone tomorrow not even a word of sorrow hoping and praying for a kiss of a mother and have a family with a sister and a brother. No laughs no joys no toys. A pack of evil men and women and all their lies. Our Little friends we made and our good memory of them soon faded.

The fear and the loneliness and the longing for a wish to be set free. I wished to enjoy my life and we happy with me we have no confidence and the insecurities of life left us broken. O why God have you forsaken us. Why are we in this hellhole our bodies all sweat and cold. Will it be my turn tonight to be taken to almighty heights? I have no say I am here a little child and I must obey every moment of everyday. When we are gone our graves will be unmarked and we will not even be known. The only joy in our hearts is to know that we will be joining mammy and daddy one day soon in the peace of God and his angels in heaven. We will then know that we have had victory and won.

For survivors of abuse

For all you little solders who have suffered come forward and tell your story of what has happen to you it is the first part of your healing and it will help you come closer to God. Many years of your life may have been stolen but don't let them take anymore. This can be the first day of the rest of your life the truth will set you free. You can live again through the Father, Son and Holy Spirit.

I praise and I thank the Lord for what he has achieved for me. The marks and the scars will always be there, but in God's love and mercy he can wash your wounds away and makes whole again.

Healing of physical handicap and mental handicap

Lord as I suffer in life I feel I have to get tougher. People laugh people mock they are around me in a flock. Look at him he is so dim. Look at her she is so grim. People have no understanding they do not know how to handle such sensitive subjects. They just inject more pain as we already feel the flame. Lord why do we stand with the fleet of mockers and do nothing about it. We have already been hit and brought down to the very pit. Lord open my heart to seek your love. Pour your precious blood over my wounds physical and mental wounds. Give people a kind word for us and a happy cheerful smile so we do not feel we do not fit in and always fighting with ourselves to win. If it is your will flow your blood though our hearts clear all the blockages and clear all the weeds and instead grow all your seeds so we can accept.

Help us to accept our disabilities and make people no longer look at disability but ability and treasure what we can do and help us to join in with them too. I lay my petition in your hands and may your will be done not mine. Take away my suffering and all my inferiority complex that I had since the beginning of my disability. I know Lord in your powers I have the ability to get better. I believe in the Father Son and Holy Spirit that they are one.

Amen

Prayer to experience God's Love

Lord make your love empower me make it grow and flow out to others so they can experience your joy and your message of hope. Take me back over my life and for every part that my mother and father lacked giving me love fill this space with your love. For all my brokeness, for all my pains and for all my losses and for all my gains fill them with your love. Show me how to love you Lord. Teach me your way and teach me your words. Give me guidance and direction so I can love you with a perfect love which will drive out all evil. Lord be the love of my life and let me be the love of yours. Together we can be friends and show the world what love is.

Amen

A Millionaire
with the Love of Jesus

I came across a heroin addict in the summer of 2000. He wore a very warm overcoat, which I thought strange, but he said he had felt so cold while coming off the heroine that he wore it day and night. He told me that he had fought the addiction through faith in Jesus and had never seen a Doctor but had gone to the Divine Physician instead.

He had grown up without any religion; his Father had none and his Mother was no longer Church of England, but someone had told him about Jesus. Then, when I looked into his eyes, I was completely taken aback because his eyes were so full of love that it was like looking at Jesus. I laid hands on him and he had such a great emotional healing that we laughed, cried and prayed together. I had never experienced such love in my life and I told him I was jealous. He said, 'Eileen, I am nothing. Just look at me and tell me why you say that'. I told him that he was a millionaire with the love of Jesus. He has now returned to work in England and has a deep religious faith.

The Power and the
Mercy of Jesus

In 2001 I had a phone call from a friend who lives in New York and he told me that his wallet had been stolen. In it had been his passport, green card, bank security card, union number and various important phone numbers. He was so upset that he could see no purpose in living; he was unable to work and could not get home. I told him to pray and ask God to work a miracle as God has the power to do anything if we trust in His Divine mercy and love.

My friends and I prayed very hard for him and he stayed home from work himself the next day and went to a church. The following morning he reported for work and explained how his wallet had been stolen with his union number in it. While he was talking, a girl with a Spanish American accent rang and asked if they knew of Sean Lynch, a union member. She had been walking through a park in Manhattan when she saw a wallet and various bits of paper on the ground, by a bin. When she had picked them up there were his passport, wallet, green card and bank and union numbers. The only thing missing was his money. He was overjoyed and now believes that God has the power to do anything.

God has the power to pull us through any situation, no matter how difficult it is. All we have to do is trust Him.

MY HORRENDOUS CHILDHOOD

Even though my horrendous childhood is all in the past, and I have learned to move on, at times it can come across in my personality when someone upsets me. God has healed me layer by layer and He is still healing me. Sometimes I can be taken right back to the hour, the moment and the day and I ask myself how I coped? But, 'when we are weak He is strong'. I could never think that that life was mine because at times it seemed so far away. Lord, have mercy on my mother now. I hope she is happy; at times in life I felt sorry for her, as she must have been so unhappy herself to treat me the way she did. She caused me such hardship not only by the way she treated me but also by the way I learned to put myself down; so it was a double cruci-fixion. I have let go of that behaviour now, thank God. When you are a child you learn certain behaviour from your parents or your guardians, whether it's good or bad. At times I thought I had acquired my learned behaviour from my mother, at others that I must have been born with it because she was like that.

I used to think my behaviour was very abnormal and the way people used to look at me would make me feel uncomfortable. Maybe it was my own imagination or I could have been para-noid because my mother was a very paranoid person and her own anxiety might have affected me. I would often come out with different things to what other people would say so I never thought my opinion was valuable. That's the way things were until I had my independence. Up to this stage I was trapped into a way of thinking. If you learn to do a new task it takes time. After many attempts you get it right and eventually you become perfect at it and it becomes easier. I was not allowed to explore my own mind in the way I wanted. So for a period of my life that part of me did not develop and I was emotionally stunted. It was like not having a mind of my own and part of me was shut in a box and put away. When I was eventually allowed to think for myself I was an amateur at it. I had learned my bad behaviour and I was an expert. Many books are written today and this is one area that is not highlighted much. It is very important because such people might go through their lives having no social abilities or confidence and their development could be impaired in hundreds of ways.

I thank God that He healed me and set me free. I know people today who had similar lives to me, and now, 20 years further on, they still feed and nourish themselves with the bad behaviour they learned from their parents. These unhealthy thoughts, or feelings of inferiority, have controlled their lives and, instead of breaking free of them when they left whatever home they had, they still carry them. As a result, today they are very unhappy people. Even though those who over- powered them or who manipulated them have gone, they are still in the hands of those who made them suffer; they will have these scars for life unless they break free.

Changing our way of thinking is very important as it can make you a new person with a better quality of life. These unhappy thoughts are not healthy for our brains and can make people very depressed and make them suffer from low self-esteem. In the Lords name I praise Him for setting me free.

GOSSIP AND HOW IT
DESTROYS RELATIONSHIPS

When I was a child I lived near a small village and the greatest place for gossip was the pub. People who did not hear the local news got all their information, wrong or right, in the pub.

It is funny but you always hear from gossips the bad news, about the bad things that people have done; you rarely hear about the good. Some people always like to hear the bad story. If someone dies in the community, usually people find something good to say about him. It is sad that we have to wait for someone to die before anything nice is said about him or her.

What really gets to me is, why did they not help those people out when they were alive, or, as I call it, show neighbourly love. Why did they waste their energy in the pub gossiping and criticising their fellow man when they could use that energy to do good, and help someone in trouble and lend him or her a hand. I always think about what Jesus said in scripture, ' Let the man that is without sin cast the first stone'. What makes me laugh is this, that there is no such thing as a first stone. It is a constant stone, thrown at a particular person. If a man wins money, or gets a promotion at work, people will automatically say, 'he or she has enough', instead of being happy, and wishing them well. They are jealous and are full of envy, and wish it had been them.

Think of a flower which is dying, or a rose with its flowers dead, the petals about to fall off; if someone does not prune back the rose, the energy will still be going into the dead flowers instead of producing new stems. This is energy that is wasted instead of being creative and helping someone. Actions speak louder than words. When I see people gossiping, I think of a rosebush with the flowers dying.

The media today is run on bad news; it is what sells the papers and makes the country work. The bad news is run by the power of Satan. He is able to manipulate people's minds. Some of what we read is not always accurate. Jesus is the good news. As it says in scripture, ' let him who is thirsty come'; 'with joy let us draw waters from the wells of salvation'. Some people today are not listening to scripture, and are drawing unclean water from the wrong source to quench their thirst.

By gossiping we take away a person's character, and we give them an image that other people judge them by. Even if they are innocent, people still look on them as if they are guilty. Taking a person's character is like taking a person's life. A tongue is like a match which can set a whole forest on fire; once it happens it is never quenched. An unpleasant story stays with people, but the good story or good words only last for a short period. Gossip is soul destroying, so we should pray more and talk less.

If you put two strangers in a waiting room it is nearly always the bad news that gets people chatting. I am not disputing the fact that good stories are also told but they are not usually in the majority. If they were following God, when these people heard the bad news their hearts would be filled with compassion, and they would not judge. They would pray for the victim who was suffering and grieving; they would give their full concentration to building new bridges and new roads for their neighbours to cross. We should always reach out with love. In my own case some people knew that I was suffering, some relations must have known that Mother was giving me a very hard life but they just turned a deaf ear, and thought it best not to interfere. I might have been judged as a bad person as a child, as mother often gave out to me in public.

One day when I was in a shop in the local town, the shop was crowded with people. The owner of the shop handed me a bun; I was overjoyed, as I was hungry. Mother immediately gave out to me in front of everyone, and I felt that I was unworthy to eat it. I wanted the owner to take back the bun, but she refused. I felt the whole shop was gossiping about me and I could not understand the reason.

In the past, as you know, people always thought parents were right rather than the child; nowadays, thank God, they favour the child. Parents are judged by how they care for their children. If we ever hear a story of someone in trouble, especially a child, because they are so vulnerable, it is our duty to do something to help him or her. We must get him out of the situation, especially if he is being abused or is suffering at the hands of others. He may have no one else to help him and we should use our knowledge wisely. We should forget about ourselves, even if we have to put ourselves at risk, to save some person or some child.

When we are in trouble, if Jesus were to turn His back on us, how would we feel? We need to lean on one another and let God be our unity. We should start today and talk about the good, and stop criticising. When we do not know the full circumstances of a person's trouble, and if we cannot help them directly for some reason, we should pray that God would put someone in their way.

It only takes one person to change the habit of gossiping and speak well of people. After a while, when people see that putting others down is not tolerated, they too will change because they will have no one to listen to them. One thing people do not understand is that bad news can depress people and even make one sick. It can really upset some people, because they can relate it to a situation in their past. It can open wounds and cause a lot of emotional upsets. For example, a group of young teenagers might be talking about abuse, not realising that there is an abused teen among them and the others would not understand that person's sensitivity to the subject.

We should choose our words, and speak well of everyone. We should focus on the good things in life, and let God be the judge. Attitude is more important than facts. We should think positively and our hearts should be full of love, understanding, empathy and loyalty to those who need us. We can aim at making the world a better place, and in our hearts will grow seeds, that will be forever rooted in the heart of God. Jesus said ' What you do to others, you do to me'. See Jesus in everyone because we are all brothers and sisters in Christ.

Open my eyes Lord,
I want to see Jesus

Many times in life, I have felt the force in opposition, which is evil. When I am going about my daily business, or doing the work of God I just need to take a look at a person's eyes, or an animal's eyes, to see evil, 'Our eyes are the lamps of our soul'. I try and rebuke the evil and say, 'In Jesus name be gone', and then feel my paths clear so that I can walk, knowing that God's wonderful works have been performed.

At other times when I feel the force coming against me, it can be so wicked that I feel my whole body is chained. I feel as if I am in a prison and that I need to be released. When I am released, I feel peace and joy and it is as if the darkness of hell has been closed, and the fire of God's light opened. Sometimes I feel suffering for no reason, just because I pass a place that has an evil history; again, I need to be unlocked.

When you become open to God, your Spirit becomes sensitive, and you can discern between good and evil. It is God inspiring us with His Holy Spirit, so that we can be guided. God gives us wisdom and knowledge, which keeps us on His path; He is our water that never stops flowing.

Once He has started you on a journey, He will give you the strength to complete it, until you go to your eternal resting-place. God is your strength, your rock and your stronghold. He will see you through, with His wonderful gifts, and the fruits of the Holy Spirit. You will be nourished by His words, and you will grow in His Holy Spirit.

There is no such thing as total maturity in the Spirit, because you will mature in it, until the day you die. The longer you grow, the more your eyes will be opened. You will see things the way God sees them.

When our eyes are opened, it is like a seal from God, for our protection, so we do not go back to our old way of life. The longer that you are in the Spirit, the more you can be under evil attack. The evil one will do anything to bring you back to the life when you did not know God. You can spend years building towers, or growing in the Spirit and even half a lifetime following God but when you let go the hand of God, all that you gained, over a long period of time, can be lost quickly. You only have to be a couple of weeks back in your old life, of not following God, and these ways will stay with you. You will forget what your life with God was like, and what you had achieved when you were with God, the joy, the peace, and the happiness you felt. Living a life of immorality causes people, to be depressed, to be in sorrow, and many more things.

Training is the key to staying with God; practice praying from your heart because practice makes perfect. Behave just like a sportsman who needs to keep training in order to become fit. You build on what you have, which is today, and put your whole past life behind you. If you can wake up with the attitude that the Lord has blessed you with another day, and then say to yourself,' I will do his work to the best of my ability, without sinning', then you are following God. God has given us the strength to say no when we are tempted. Expelling temptations is a virtue of God.

The way of life that we live can become like an addiction. No one wants change or to be changed but we must admit to ourselves that we are weak and He is strong. When we do this we rely on His strength, not our own. So follow God and every day will be a happy song.

24 HOURS

In twenty-four hours, the world can change,
Life on earth, to good, can be rearranged.
If it was only for a minute or two, united in prayer,
What a world we would have, it would be so fair.
One hand cannot be with God, and the other somewhere else,
It is all or nothing. To walk with God you must surrender yourself.
You are spiritual beings, by the Divine God you were constructed,
And by His love if you follow Him, you are conducted.
When you were made by His power, you were perfect,
By the infestation of sin, you have become sick, and infected.
Everything can change in a matter of minutes.
Follow your Divine leader, not the false gods you have made senators,
By following them, you have given them great popularity,
But remember, love your neighbour, and help those that need charity.
Love of money causes people to become greedy,
When instead, we should draw on God's power to help the needy.
Some people help others only to look important in the public eye,
Through their severe manipulation, others believe in their lies.
Our government is an example of this when it comes to voting time,
If we don't vote in their favour, we feel it is a crime,
We think we will be forgotten in times of trouble,
And without their help we feel our world will crumble.
Through our own lack of faith in God, we can be really let down,
And by following hypocrites, we can lose our sense of what is sound,
With God we never fail, because He is true to His word,
And if everyone turned to Him, we would have a beautiful world.

THE POWER OF JESUS

I went to Dublin 3 weeks ago and before I left the house, the Holy Spirit inspired me to take 3 photographs of the garden with me. I met a lady on the train and she said her heart was very troubled. Her only daughter was going out with a Muslim who seemed to have complete control over her and didn't want her to have anything to do with her family. She said she had very little faith in God as she felt He was not answering her prayers. I prayed with her and she said she felt a load lifting from her heart, that it was a miracle and that she felt wonderful. I then gave her a photo of the garden and told her about all the wonderful healings that are taking place there. She was overjoyed and promised to pay a visit to the garden.

I then met a lady from Australia in a cafe, whose husband works in Dublin. She said she had been to Medjugorge and was very interested in visiting holy places. I gave her a photo of the garden and she was fascinated and said she hoped to visit it shortly.

Thirdly, I met a homeless man who was very bitter and suicidal. He said that his wife and children had walked out on him and that he was very depressed. I told him to pray, and gave him a small sum of money to tide him over. Finally I gave him the third picture of the garden and this was the one with the special crucifix. I told him Jesus also suffered rejection and pain when He was on the cross. The man's face changed and I could see softness underneath the anger and the hurt. We talked for some time and then he went off much more peaceful and happy.

Across the Shadows of my Life

All my life I have loved light, natural light. It is as if, for most of my childhood, I was working down in the mines. I was like the man who says in the song, ' At the age of 60, never again will I go down underground`; that is I. It might have taken me many years to come into the light but, now that I am, I never again want to go into the dark. Jesus is my light, and my salvation. Those that are in the light see things in the light, and those that are in the dark see the things in the dark.

From the moment, the Holy Spirit, enlightened me, I was lit up. I do not know whether it was a forty watt or a hundred watt bulb, but light is light. It is the light that will never go out. The bulb will never blow, because it is the eternal light. The light is the way that god thinks and inspires your mind. You have to be melted and remoulded from the dark of the past, before you are part of the light.

A mirror can only reflect the images that it is shown such as beauty, disaster, or evil. My mirror reflected pain, hope and deprivation. When I looked in the mirror that is what I saw. Not a beautiful little girl, with brown hair, but a little girl who was not loved or cared for but a hatred for the shadow that should have reflected light. The light was like a halo; the inside was dark and empty. My mirror only reflected this, when I looked into it. At all other times, there was no mirror, as all the pain was locked inside. I had no way of expressing myself, only dark clouds around me.

Today when I look in the mirror, I see me and how wonderful I am, in God's image; the way he made me. There is nothing trapped, as I can see who I am. God is my mirror that reflects, love, joy, peace and hope.

BEHIND THE TRUTH LIES A TERRIBLE PAST

Behind the truth lies a terrible past. It is funny how our lives reflect the life of Jesus and hard to believe how we follow Jesus, through different ways. Jesus said, 'If you want to be a disciple of mine follow me', and it is amazing how our lives follow Him, before we reach the truth. It is what we do with the truth that changes our lives. I was once a captive but now I am free. Free to preach the word of God and free to do His works. If I did not have a past I would not have the love I now have for God. So really, when you think about it, even having a past seems a failure it's not a failure if you can turn it around and that goes for everyone. My past, you could say, was a failure because of the way I suffered; it was not the glory of God at work but it was the hand of God that turned my life around. We are born to praise the glory of God. God has a covenant with us before we are born. We are His children and in Him only shall we trust. It is wonderful to have received the message of God because it helped me.

When I think of countries where God is not known, it makes me sad. They have horrendous lives without any hope. It is the hope that keeps us sane, and gives us the will to live. It lifts the burdens off our shoulders and sets us free. People do not realise the value of hope. Even if what we dream about does not come true, at least we can still look forward to a future of peace, prosperity and freedom in hope. The rose of hope, just like the flower itself when it is in season, yields to God and flowers with glory. Its testing time is during the hardship of winter and the frost and that is the way my life has been. I was a briar and now I am a rose in colour and in season. Praise the Lord, Alleluia! The Lord has fed me with His word, month by month, year by year. His word is my food and nourishment. Just as with the flower blossoming, I sometimes feel like a flower as it does in the winter and I ask myself, 'where is God` but he is always at my side, not far away. God is a God of love, he gives us love and in love we grow

THE INNOCENT ROSE

One morning a little rose bud opened to yield to the sun,
It opened its petals, so beautiful in colour, one by one,
Absorbing all the nourishment from earth it could take.
That's was the reason from its sleep it became awake,
It smelt like perfume that was so sweet,
 And every moment of its life was God's beat.
In the cold it shrivelled up and went back to sleep,
And in those days it stayed humble and meek,
Waiting for the sun. It was very patient,
Trusting in the Lord it had no hesitation,
Never complaining, doing what it was told
 Because the little flower knew it was God's mould.
If we were all little flowers we would have seasoning,
And to our lovely God we would be very pleasing.
We would not mind being cold or even freezing,
Because, during our trials, God would give us easing.
When you think of a flower think of yourself and others,
Tell them of the flowers so that they too can be your brothers.

SOME EXPERIENCES OF EVIL SITUATIONS

When I was five years old I started school. It was a very small, damp old building and the only form of heating was an open fire. I felt so proud, walking down the dusty road in my new shoes and a lovely strawberry pink suit that my Mammy had knitted for me. There were no tar roads in rural Ireland in 1943, except for a few main roads.

As I kicked the stones down the steep hill I felt really happy until I had to pass a certain laneway and I instantly felt a fear that sent shivers down my spine. After some time I mentioned it to my Father and, after looking at me in astonishment, he sat me down beside him and told me how Mary Ring, the witch, used to live there. Apparently, Grandfather always used to try and stay on good terms with her because he was afraid that she would commit some evil act. She had put curses and spells on many people; when my Father was young she had cursed their farm and they had had no cream on their milk for a year. She used to bury dead animals, hens and eggs in farmers' fields. Any form of black magic is evil, including fortune telling, tarot cards and new age practices.

The Devil is trying today to influence our youth with satanic music that often glorifies drug abuse, murder, suicide and Satanism. 'Black metal' lyrics are obsessed with death, violence and satanic imagery. All witches, whether black or white, worship Satan; white witches are simply those who convince people that they only tell them good things. That is just a way of deceiving them. When you worship God you become full of joy, love and peace, whereas when you worship Satan you are filled with hatred, despair and unhappiness and are inspired to destroy other lives.

Returning Home from Boston

In 1994 I had a beautiful holiday in Boston with my daughter and grandchild and we stayed with my son Brian. It was autumn and the colours of the trees were magnificent. In their red, orange and yellow foliage the beauty of God's creation was so clear. As we were rushing to catch a plane, I looked someone who was going in the opposite direction straight in the eye. Immediately I experienced an evil force coming towards me and I felt so weak and sick that I had to struggle hard to climb into the plane. I prayed very hard and at one stage thought I was going to pass out.

Eventually I got my strength back as Jesus is our strength and our rock to lean on, ' I can do all things through Christ who strengthens me '. This man was involved in Satanism and God revealed it to me. As it says in scripture, ' our eyes are the lamps of our soul'.

Driving Through West Cork

One beautiful, sunny evening in late summer 2001, my son asked me to go for a drive with him in the country. We visited the historic town of Kinsale, situated on the south coast of Ireland and known for its narrow streets, magnificent seafood restaurants and picturesque scenery.

Next we took the coast road to Clonakilty and when we approached a crossroads, a short distance from the town, I felt an evil force and prayed for deceased souls who were murdered there during the troubled times in Ireland. As we drove on towards Dunmanway I could hear the birds singing and giving glory to God. It is wonderful how nature does this; you can see a herd of cows in a field and, all of a sudden, they raise their heads to adore their creator. How much more praise should we give Him as we are created in His image? Then we went up a small road and, all of a sudden, I felt an evil force so strong that I could hardly breathe. The Holy Spirit revealed to me that slaves were tortured at that spot thousands of years ago.

A BEAUTIFUL NEW BUNGALOW

A young couple called John and Rose married and built a bungalow on John's Father's land. They were a very happy couple but after a time I noticed that Rose had become very depressed and was particularly hard on her children. Her personality had completely changed. I prayed for happiness for them all and it was revealed to me that animals and children had been tortured and killed there many, many years ago. I fetched some holy water and baptised them one by one, in the name of the Father, Son and Holy Spirit.

When Jesus was telling me some of the children's names I could feel the awful suffering. One child, by the name of Rose, had been tortured in horrific ways. The bungalow had been built on the exact location of a graveyard, which was why Rose had been so depressed. I found a priest to say prayers for exorcism and mass was said in the house.

SHARING IS CARING

Jesus taught us in scripture how to share. In John 6.verse 6.
' when Jesus saw the great crowd coming towards him. He said to Philip ' Jesus only said this to test him' For he already had in mind what to do. Philip, Peter's brother said, " Here is a little boy, with two small fish and five barley loaves" Jesus then worked a wonderful miracle. The little boy could have been self-ish and kept then for himself.

Jesus worked a miracle, and five thousand were fed. Twelve baskets were filled with the leftovers. Jesus was trying to teach us the important of sharing, and how later He was going to share His body with the gift of the Eucharist.

As I have said preciously Ireland was totally different in my childhood to what it is today. We lived a humble, simple lifestyle, and left our problems to God. Money was scarce, but everyone helped each other. As a child if I got an apple, I shared it with my friend. The same went for lollipops. It was not very hygienic, but sharing came first in our lives.

I remember one day reading a story about Mother Theresa of Calcutta. Mother Theresa is now a canonised saint. She will always be remembered for her service to the poorest of the poor. One day she entered a home where an old lady had not eaten for two days. Mother Theresa gave her food consisting of rice and vegetable. When she was not eating it, mother Theresa became curious. Then the little lady looked up and said to her " Do you mind if I share it with another lady, who lives two doors up, be-cause she has not eaten either for two days.

As the saying goes, the poor are rich and the rich are poor. The poor can teach us a lot about sharing. With the rich it is all me. That is why we have so many lonely people among the well off. We have single people who live on their own in our cities. They pretend they do not need anyone. They boast of their independ-ence. Deep down they are miserable. Through life we all need one another.

Loneliness is like cancer in our society today. We were all made for community. That is where the word communion comes from. If you walk into a moll, in any of our supermarkets, you will find people strolling about, waiting for someone to talk to.

I met a lot of those lonely people in America. America is known as a country of opportunity, so a lot of people migrate there from the poorer countries. I met some of those immigrants in restaurants, and they told me they found it hard to adapt to a different culture, and how they missed their families and friend.

One day I was strolling, through 'the commons' in Boston, when I saw this old lady sitting on a bench. She looked lonely and lost. I sat beside her, and she instantly got into deep conversation. She began to tell me her life story, and her fascination for money, and how she possessed all different currencies. While I was chatting with her, she offered me money. I immediately got the impression that she was offering me money, just for speaking to her. I chatted for awhile, and then she invited me to her apartment. I had to refuse as I had a train to catch. I could feel her loneliness as I was leaving her. When we put our trust in money, it will not make us happy. As it says in scripture 'The love of money is the root of all evil'

When I was training to be a nurse, I worked in a small hospital. The first floor was for private patients, who had very few visitors, and often complained of being lonely. The second floor was in sharp contrast to the first floor. This floor had two large wards. Each patient was always watching out for the next, and always ready to seek help for them, if they needed it. They were never lonely and always had lots of visitors.

I will always remember one evening, a lady was dying in her bed, she had all her family and friends around her. Her son was ordained to the priesthood a few weeks previous. He was asked to administer the sacrament of the sick. When he anointed her head with oil, he began to cry. Then all family and friends started to cry. I then cried also, which was not very professional, but I was overcome, when I saw the young priest cry. It just goes to show you that sharing in grieve is so important. When Jesus was on His way to be crucified. When He saw a crowd of women who were weeping, it gave Him great comfort, as compassion and mercy are part of life.

REACH FOR THE STARS

Reach for the stars, no matter who you are,
Get over the division, make God's desire your decision,
He is up there in the sky, asks no questions or the reason why.
Accept that He made you unique, better than any boutique,
Listen to His words; do not strike with a sword
If you are down, there is only one way up with a crown,
He is your narrator, listen to your dictator,
He gives with love; The Holy Spirit is His dove,
He can set you free, and fill your heart with glee.
Love your neighbour, because God will give you favour;
About your deeds do not boast, because Jesus is your host,
He is your salvation, and you live in His creation,
He will wipe your eyes, and make you wise.
In your life he will pick the stones, and give you a happy tone,
Reach for the stars whoever you are,
You can not go there by car; it is different to the human bizarre,
You will be dancing; your soul and spirit will be enhancing;
O, blessed God, help me say your road I trod,
I raise my hands in prayer; you are my God who is always there.

A JOURNEY TO CALVARY

We should really forget about ourselves, and concentrate on the bigger picture. We should make the Stations of the Cross with Jesus, and go through each station, one by one. When we hear of other people's troubles, our own then seem small. By going through the stations with Jesus, we will be able to feel the suffering of the inner child, and we can then cry out our own.

When we think of the suffering of Jesus at each station, it gives us hope. Our suffering, united to Jesus, is called surrender. When we do this, the love of God floods our channels and our hearts become open to receive blessings, healing and grace. We can hold the hand of Jesus and ask Him to put us in His arms. At every station we will find a situation that is reflected in our own lives.

Jesus said share your heart and your words with mine, I can fulfil any wish, any dream, if it is accordance with my Father's will. Jesus said, 'Nothing is impossible to God'. Jesus' words are forever, and what He said two thousand year ago, still stands in today's society. I think the words that were used in prophecy actually affect people more today than they did two thousand years ago.

If your heart bleeds from despair, get your bible, and ask Jesus to use your hands to give you a reading that will lift you up and empower you. You will then, be released from worry, and your stress and anxiety will go away.

As you go through the Stations of the Cross, you will feel very close to Jesus, and you will feel bad if you offend Him. You will feel guilty for your sins. That is the awesome wonder of God. It is as if God is disciplining us on our way, so we do not stray off the track. The truth is, if you love Jesus you will go with Him and never hurt Him. Every time you sin you are giving Him another agonising death, because 'What you do to others, you do unto Me'.

Jesus said, 'If you love Me, you will keep my commandments'. A lot of people say how can you love someone whom you do not know. If you have experienced a loving, intimate relationship, you will know what I am talking about. You can fall in love with Jesus, and reach a stage where you can actually end up not hurting Him.

Your loving relationship can be so profound that a touch can be so tender, and a word used wrongly can feel like a betrayal. This closeness to Jesus begins, when you lay down your life to follow Him. Jesus loves everyone and it is His will that everyone should be saved.

He can only guide, direct and speak the words of His Father. It is up to each individual to follow Him. He inspires us, and gives us many opportunities in our lifetime to turn to Him. He even puts people in our way to guide us. Our hands and our feet are not our own, God uses our hands and feet to do his work. Christ has no body on earth now, but ours, to carry out His duties. We must say 'yes` to Him today to do His work so that good works will flourish. He might not give us our reward, today or tomorrow, but He will give it to us when we least expect it. It is just like when we least expect miracles in our lives, they suddenly happen. His hands are always waiting to lift us up, out of every situation. Jesus is with us when we are carrying all our crosses and He never gives us crosses that are too heavy to carry. His cross is our redemption. He is the Saviour of the world, His cross made a way for us to get to heaven. After every night there is a day, so you can see that suffering is not forever.

We should unite our suffering with Jesus, and he will give us the strength to carry it. ' Cast your burdens on to me, for I am meek and humble of heart'. When we follow Jesus, we lay down our crosses, as He is 'The way, the truth and the life'. When we depend on our own strength, to get through our suffering, we are fighting an unending battle with ourselves. Suffering is the start of our journey to getting to know God. It makes us humble. God is the solution to all of our problems. Some people do not ask for help from God, but when everything else fails, they use Him as a last resort. Remember God is the everlasting Divine physician that heals all your wounds.

Trust in the Lord who is so kind, and in your soul, and you will have peace of mind.

STEPPING OUT IN FAITH

On the 17th of Dec 2004, I got a phone call inviting me to speak to a group of alcoholics in a treatment centre in Armagh. I decided to go on the 17th of January and bed and breakfast was arranged for me. Someone was also supposed to meet me off the train in Newry, and drive me to Armagh. On the 16th of January I got a phone call from the lady who was supposed to collect me, who told me that she had to rush to England to a funeral, as a relative had died. I decided to step out in faith, and I knew that if I trusted in God, and did not doubt, that everything would be O.K. Then to make matters worse, I had a phone call from the lady, who was going to keep me for the night. She was ill and had to go to the doctor. I knew that Jesus wanted me to go and visit the centre and I knew that they were expecting me, so I felt that I could not let them down. I handed it all over to Jesus, just like a child hands her life over to the care of her parents. A child does not worry about the electricity bill, or where the food on the table comes from.

Then the most extraordinary thing happened. About an hour later I received a phone call, from Mary Ward, who lives in Newry, 'saying she would love to meet me'. When I told her I was off to Newry the next day she and her husband arranged to meet me off the train and then took me to their home and gave me something to eat. Next, I prayed with their family and relations. I was just about to leave when I met a group of drug addicts who opened up their hearts to me, and told me about their suffering because of their addiction. Some of them were separated from their wives, because they could not cope with family life. I prayed with them and God touched them powerfully; I could see an immediate change in them. I told them that God loved them to bits, and they could feel joy again, and a wish to carry on, as all drug addicts have suicidal tendencies. Then I realised why I had to go to Newry.

I decided to go by bus to Armagh and when I got there, I enquired from the bus driver, as to the whereabouts of the treatment centre. He was so kind, and he said, 'Come with me, quickly', and walked with me, almost right into the centre. I praised and thanked God for everything. When I began my talk to the group of alcoholics, I was overwhelmed by the welcome they gave me. I then realised how close to God they were. As scripture says, 'God is very close to the broken hearted, whose spirits are crushed'.

It was now 8 p.m. and I had nowhere to sleep. I just had not had time to look for accommodation. Then a phone call came to the centre from a lady saying she would gladly put me up for the night if I had not arranged anything already. This was a lesson for me, to trust completely in God and not to doubt Him.

THE 7 STEPS OF SALVATION

Lord Jesus take me back over my life to heal my brokenness and unforgiveness. I desire you to do this Lord and to direct me on the path of life. You are my rock, my strength and my salvation. Been as strong as a rock I can confide in you and trust you and my earthly life will never fall apart. Your strength Lord means I can draw from you, the light of your glory and the healing you desire me to have. Salvation means Lord you will teach me how to pray and follow your word, so I can live a life of prayer and never be lead astray.

I ask you Lord to make me humble and I ask you with an open heart to heal the wounds of my past. Lord Jesus I place all my trust in you to take me back to my mother's womb. Heal me of all the negativity that my mother had in conceiving me. Heal all the injuries I may have received in my mother's hard labour. Now Lord will you please walk with me during the first year of my life. Heal me of all the temper tantrums and all my embarrassing moments I had. Heal me of the wounds that I got because my sisters and brothers were unkind to me.

Now Jesus hold my hand and walk with me through the first five years of my life, please heal me of any physical injuries I got because of falls and physical abuse. Heal me of my relationship I had with my parents because they found me difficult, heal me of the shame I felt about my body and please heal me of my inferiors I had when I first started school. Heal me of any bullying I received because I was different from my other schoolmates and heal me of any other things Lord I need healing in during these first five years.

Next Lord please carry me from five to ten years, heal me of any negativity I had about myself as I began to grow. Heal me of the lack of trust I had in you. Heal me of my parent criticism. Help me Lord to forgive my brothers and sisters for the fights they had with me. Now Lord as I become independent forgive me for not been modest about the clothes I wore. Forgive me for the anger I had towards my parents and for been disobedience.

Help me to forgive my teachers for emotional trauma they cause me. Now Lord I hand these people over to you and help me to forgive them with a sincere loving heart, because love is the greatest gift you gave me Lord and you want me to use it in special ways.

Now Lord take me into the boat over the sea of Galilee and may I rest there with you so you can heal me of the next ten years, these were the most difficult times of my life and the memories still flood me. I am in the boat with you Lord the wind is high I should place all my trust in you because the boat is rocking, never forsake me from the boat Lord I need you to heal my memories of sexual fantasies, Bullying, bad video and any thing that is object-able to you Lord. Heal me of the jealousy I felt about my friends I thought they were more beautiful than I was.

Heal me of all the petty crimes I committed that only you know. I ask you to forgive me for not drawing from your source of strength and not confiding in you because I can not do things alone without you Lord. Thank you Lord for healing me of the first twenty years of my life.

Now Lord I place my trust in you, to walk through the rest of my life with me for all the sins I committed and all the offences I caused you O' My Lord My God. I now believe Lord that you have physical, mentally and emotionally healed me. You said Lord that believing is receiving and you alway keep your prom-ises. I am now happy Lord to follow you and give my life over to you so you can use me as a tool to save others.

Thank you for the gift of faith and all the other gifts you gave me. Now Lord I lay down my life to you and rest in you and obey your words. You are the redeemer, healer and consoler of my life. I am now converted and I go into the world to proclaim your good news. You are doing the work Jesus, and I am here your earthly tool. Praise the Lord for His works.

Amen

THE UPLIFTING FATHER

Now that I draw my book to a close,
I hope all you who read it will feel God's love flow;
Chapter by chapter it is now down to history,
As you can see God's miracles in life are a mystery.
What He has done for me He can do for you,
Just stay on His path and follow as He told you to,
Through sorrow and despair you will find He is there,
Because He is the Lord who really loves you and cares.
My story is a guideline for those who know no other way,
And your life can be turned around if you trust in Him today.
Your future will be of love, joy, peace and hope,
He will show you the way to climb up the rope.
Your hearts will be filled with gladness and peace,
Jesus will be living in you so you will feel His presence increase,
You will grow bigger according to the truth,
And by following Him you will be part of His fruits.
A fruit that will bring good harvest and never sour,
So overcome everything with Jesus and grow like a tower.
God is inspiring and He does all the uplifting,
And in your heart the sorrow will be shifting.
Trust in Him and you will have a new life for eternity,
Because now you can unlock heaven with the Divine key.

My life today

Now today that I put all my suffering behind God uses me as a tool to heal others. I can relate to other people's suffering because of my own life. Mother died in 1990, and for years I prayed for her that she would be happy and released from her suffering.

It is important for all of you out there who are suffering because of other people. Start praying to God for those people so they get conversion. Pray for everyone who has hurt you that they will find happiness because people who are hurt themselves hurt others.

Do not go through life thinking that there is no way out as Jesus is alive

With Jesus you have nothing to fear and if you don't become involved with Him you will never know what He has in store for you. You must remove the blockages that stop the power of God's loving mercy flowing through you. The blockages are unforgiveness, revenge hatred, guilt and fear. Pray unceasingly to get your requests answered.

My Confusion to
My Everlasting Conclusion

To draw my story to a conclusion, life has been full of disappointments, joys and surprises. My disappointments are what really led me to God. My joy is what helps me to praise Him. My surprises and miracles lead me to give Him great homage, glory, and praise. Life can be bitter, and sweet. When I taste the bitter, I taste the pits of darkness. My life has been a journey, of love and compassion, with a glorified God. He brightens my way, and puts a lamp on my path. He uses the edge of His sword to keep evil away. It was also a journey of discovery, and for my lost life a recovery.

God has given me so much back into my life. I have walked on nails, and I have bled, I have walked on carpet, and felt the peace. I have met many people, some were beautiful and some were different. I have met many people in prayer, and from their knowledge, I have learned wisdom. From their testimony, I have found hope, from their fruits I have found God, who is the truth.

What I do in my life, I try to master skilfully. I try never to miss an opportunity to go in the direction that God is calling me. My dream is to fulfil God's work, and what He gives me in return is a great feeling of well being. I experience joy and a feeling I cannot explain, it is so awesome. I feel as if He is beside me, closer than I have ever felt to anyone. I am afraid at times, in case I would go the wrong way, and lose my friendship with God. What I have gained over many years of prayer, praise, and teaching could be lost quickly, if I turn my back, and let go of the hand of God. It can take a long time again, to reach that stage of growth, and maturity in the Spirit.

God is my tree, and I am His branch, and I hope other people reading this book, will be touched by the hand of God, because we are all part of the family of God.

A message I give to all, if you are disappointed with life look at yourself and smile. Feel the smile going through your being, and say one day it will be over. It will not last forever; it is only a milestone. Life is full of ups and down, crowns and frowns. We all experience them and so too, did Jesus. If you have got the joy of the Holy Spirit, dance in it, and take your reward. What you will experience is an everlasting peace that will never bring you down.

If you are someone who is wise and knowledgeable there is no stage at which you will stop growing. There is no such thing as reaching your peak with prayer and praise.

If you have the gift of knowledge, do not keep it to yourself. Go out and spread the good news. Bad news travels fast, so let the good news travel rapidly. Melt, remould the broken and help them to unfold their problems. They may look you in the eye and laugh but soon they will realise they are powerless, without the greatest force on earth.

I hope all of you, who read the book, realise that God is active, like a handyman. When you feel that your joy is fading, remember that what He has done for others He can do for you. He has done wonders in my life. But do not wait for a moment of struggling to turn to Him. Turn to Him, before the world might come crashing down. He will then make you fit and able during those hard times. Jesus can intervene on your behalf to avoid certain situations and crises. He is a God who shares and cares, who knows your heart and your mind. He is nearer than the door; He is your friend. He has no on or off peak. He is watching over you like a shepherd, and in your troubles He will be at your side like a leopard. He is a God of victory. He has won the battle. Your grounds have been freed. Let the love of God be your addiction, and your old ways that used to afflict you be gone. United to Him He will be your Saviour, and those who call on the name of Jesus already have their favours.

ME THEN AND ME NOW

When I take a glance over my life, some memories are fond, others are like a reflection on a pond, some are treasures that are enhanced and some keep close to my heart to remember it is a pleasure. Every thing in living had a beginning, a living and an end. My beginning was no singing with it no treasured memories do I bring. My beginning I had to fight for survival because of my mother's deprival, in my life she caused me many rivals. As I grew older I started to live, I was no longer the sieve. Making my own decisions was perfect I did not have to tolerate divisions, when I was free from my mother's legion. My lif3e had many boycotts, many holes just like been eaten by the moths. Being able to chose in my life was my cruise. Peacefully flowing I had no moaning. Forgiving helped me carry on living. You can live forever in your past and it will be forever a time bomb that will blast. I was now green like the grass just like God creation I was doing his task. I found God and He found me I am the branch and He is the tree. When I think of God I think of a tree and every little branch is God's children and part of His ranch. If I see a branch cut down I feel it is like taking away God's crown. Because without it the rest would not survive. Their God that was once alive in them is now dead, that why a family tree got its name. It's like the food chain and the genetic chain. What we got from our master was great pasture, and we must pass it on before it is too late before our life is gone, That's why I have the here and now I have God to make His tree grow, I help plant the seeds as they sow

A MOTHER'S LOVE

A mother leans over her cradle,
Her eyes full of love for her baby,
She prays for her bundle of joy,
 To her it is her heavenly toy.

She hugs and she kisses her baby,
She plays with her fingers and toes,
She can see the wisdom of God in her little Sadie,
As she rocks her in her cradle too and fro.

We thank God almighty for babies,
The joy the pleasure they bring,
With their giggles and wiggles and laughter,
Then a sweet lullaby the Mammy will sing.

Forget about cobwebs and dusting the house,
The baby is sleeping as quiet as a mouse,
The work will be done the house won't fall down,
So snap out of being stressed and God's peace will be found.

Your baby will grow up and have God as its Saviour,
So play now with your baby and enjoy its behaviour,
The baby depends on its mammy for its feeds,
So God and His angels help mammy with her needs.

A SAD SOUL

My smile is fake my tears are real,
From the outside world I form a seal,
Lord give me a trouble free heart without any pain,
So my life with You will not be of loss but of gain,

I cry myself to sleep at night,
No one understands why I cannot see the light,
Lord change my attitude to life,
Give me joy give peace and then I can strife.

Give me strength to walk in happiness,
Whether at home in school or in the bus,
Help me to laugh and sing a song,
With a merry joyful heart all day long.

ALL CREATURES GREAT AND SMALL

God made every creature great and small,
Every heart has a calling,
Every heart He made has love,
Even the Holy Spirit that He chose as a dove.

Jesus loves His flower,
Even these praise His power,
He made the briars even the nettles,
On every plant he gave petals.

He gave manpower but what man has sown is sour,
Harvest has taken disease life is no longer at ease,
Sin is what leads to sorrow
And it takes away the lasting peace of tomorrow.

Jesus still loves His world and His creation,
Because remember He is the Mason,
Everything in it He did built,
And every cup he did fill.

Prayer can change everything,
And starting again the world can sing,
With Joy, Love Happiness and peace,
The world can once again be at ease.

ANXIETY

Anxiety in the heart cause depression,
So get rid of it it today and throw it out in the bin,
If you let it get hold of you it will fill you with stress,
And then you cannot live your life to the best.

Why carry this worry and trouble to bed,
Be happy to hand it over to Jesus instead,
He is our Father, who knows what is best,
He likes all of His children to take plenty of rest.

Be happy and joyful when put to the test,
And Jesus will lift you over the fence,
He is a God of love and mercy,
So trust and sing a song and be merry

CHRISTMAS

I love Christmas it is full of cheer,
Another year gone and a new one is near,
So put Christ back in Christmas,
And please cut out the Xmas.

It should be a time of joy love and peace,
So all quarrying and sorrow should cease,
So soak in the peace of Bethlehem,
Just image what it was like on this beautiful night,

Mary and Joseph were so full of joy,
On that fist Christmas night so long ago,
The King of peace, joy and love,
Came down to the earth from heaven above,

We should thank and praise Him for what He has done,
Like the shepherds and kings, who did one by one,
Feasting and drinking and having fun,
Is fine if we think of how it all begun.

Put prayer back into Christmas,
And realise what it's all about,
So sing praises of thanksgiving,
And in Him do not doubt.

CONVERSION

Please lord teach me to convert,
To give up my old ways and to change my heart,
You gave us commandments a long time ago,
To help us and to save us as we go too and fro.

I want to live your Life Jesus but sometimes I fall,
So walk into my life sweet Jesus and help me listen to Your call,
Help me to understand you in my life and teach me to love,
Heal me and cure me with the sacred powers from above.

In your name what is evil in my life I bind,
The future is yours and the clock of love I wind,
Flow through me with your most precious blood,
Sent down by the Holy Spirit, which brings only good.

DUTY

It is our duty to work and be honest to our master,
Unless we are sick or sore or in plaster,
It is our duty to pray and practice good works,
And share the miracles of the giving of His hands.

It is our duty to bury the dead and let them rest,
So the Lord can work with them and do His best,
It is our duty to love God the Father, Son and Holy Spirit,
So that one-day heaven we will inherit.

It is our duty to be truthful, honest and sincere,
And the wisdom of God we must not fear,
It is our duty to stay on the path of the good,
Because Jesus empowers us as he said he would.

FORGET YOUR OLD HATRED

The mouth of the righteous is a fountain of light,
So say your prayers and remain in God wonderful bright,
Violence overwhelms the mouth of the bad,
Hatred and bitterness are their thoughts going to bed.

Forgiveness is a must from the mouths of the just,
Reconcile with your enemies and forget is a must,
Malicious thoughts are in the minds of the wicked,
Revenge and pay back evil for evil is their ticket.

Hatred stored up cause dissension,
Puts love back into your heart and have satisfaction,
Jesus came to set you free and be shaken,
To get you back the years the locusts have taken.

GOD'S UNFAILING LOVE

May your unfailing love come to me O' lord,
I trust in your sacred heart and in your word,
I come to you for my salvation,
You came on earth to save the nation.

I put my hope in you and I do not despair,
When I am down and out you lift me up and show me you care,
I delight in your parables and gospel story,
You healed the sick and you gave comfort to the weary.

Teach me to follow you and to obey,
Because in your book there is no other way,
You are my God and I thank you with all my heart,
I worship and I adore you and your holy name I exalt.

GOOD NEWS

I read the good news,
  At home or in the pews
It fills me with gladness,
When it is read at mass.

I love the stories of what Jesus did for us,
He went up hill and down hill and never made a fuss,
He cured the cripple and the lame,
He healed the blind, the deaf and whoever came.

He thought us to love heal and forgive
And gave us the help only God can give,
He gave us commandments and thought us to strife,
For 'He is the way the truth and the life'

HAPPINESS

Happiness is infectious it's just like the flu,
We should past it on to one another not just a few,
It affects the young and the old,
The brave and the bold.

It changes your life and gives it meaning,
That's why life will change when you let the sun come beaming,
Some people envy the rich and famous,
And think that money will fill us with happiness and save us.

God came on earth to save the rich and the poor,
His first home was a stable cold and bare,
His mother and Joseph, the shepherds and kings,
All knew it was God from whom happiness brings.

HOPE

All of us in life should live in hope,
Even when things go wrong it helps us cope,
When you are up to your neck in hot water,
The hope and trust is then, all that matters.

How lucky we are to have faith and hope,
It helps the poor, the rich, the young and old,
When we fall we can start again and climb the ropes,
And because of God we can have a mighty scope.

When sickness comes as it sometimes does,
 Please do not make such an awful fuss,
There is help out there with God and His mother,
So nothing is too difficult when we have each other.

LOVE

Lord you are a God of love,
You created us to love with help from above,
Your graces drop like raindrops,
Your inspirations if we listen are never a flop.

You loved us so much You sent us Your son,
So we could go to God when our work is done,
He died for our sins and suffered death on a cross,
So we could be saved and not die at a loss.

When we are born Your love is sown as a seed,
Help us to nurture it good and not with greed,
If we love one another and both Father and Mother,
Then when we die we will be with God forever and ever

Joy

Rejoice and be glad and stop been sad,
Be happy and joyful life is not that bad,
Be chirply all day and smile on your way,
It gladdens your heart and transforms your day.

Smile and laugh it is like a transplant,
For the weary and the dreary they say they can't,
With God on your side He is full of joy,
So let your worries aside and belike a child with a new toy.

Stress is a killer it cause wrinkles and frowns,
So stop be stressed an always down,
From today it's up with smiles and laughter,
When your friends meet you they will feel better after.

My dog Bengie

If you look at my dog and his beautiful colours,
He never makes my life empty but fuller,
He gives me companionship love and attention,
With a wag of his tail what a pet I must mention.

When I call out his name he runs to me with glee,
With the look in his eyes the happiness you can see,
He needs loving and caring just like a child,
He likes to be with people who are humble and mild.

When Bengie is sick I then get the vet,
And then he is glad and no longer sad,
God loves all His animals they are all His creation,
Everything He made we should praise as a nation.

My Holy garden

I have a holy garden inspired from heaven dove,
The pictures all so colourful with coloured frames and alcoves,
The wells have healing water,
 So take a drink and praise your Master.

Crowds they come and crowds they go,
All find peace and joy,
They come in cars and buses and on foot,
Praying for healing for their soul bodies and cuts.

I love my holy garden inspired from above,
I listen to God's spirit in the form of a dove,
I thank Him and I praise Him,
For all He has done for me and I pray He does the same for them
.

Prayer

I talk to God and thank Him for all He has done for me.
He blesses me and is everything a father should be,
He guides me on the path of life,
And will take me to heaven when the time is right.

I praise His Holy Name and trust His sacred heart,
And thank Him for answered prayer whether slow or very fast,
He gave us His holy mother to help us on our way,
To teach us and to guide us while on this earth we stay.

He sends His Holy angels to guide us day and night,
All we have to do is ask and then everything is right,
We lift up our hearts in song when sometimes things go wrong,
He calms our troubled hearts and throws our worries in the sea,
So you can see what prayer can do for folk like you and me.

Saint Anthony

My friend you are so kind,
Whenever I loose something then I find,
You are always there when I call,
You help everyone small or tall.

When I phone you are at the other end,
To take me around the bends,
With you as my friend I am never afraid,
In good days or bad days they are all God made.

When I feel down and out and my cup filling up,
You send me your light to lift me up,
You have helped me in life in so many ways,
You lifted my spirit and gladden my days

Surprises

O God you are full of surprises,
For all who are faithful and true,
They come as soon as the sun rises,
They delight the human heart through and through.

You give us a reason for living,
That makes the sun shine in our eyes,
You are such a generous God,
You watch over our paths as we trot.

We thank you for all your surprises,
The greatest gift to your children you sent,
Because you dear son came on earth to redeems us,
So we now know what the love of a Father is meant.

THANK YOU JESUS

Thank you Jesus for today,
About tomorrow I have no say,
Thank you for my lovely friends,
With them I do not have to make amends.

Thank you for the love of my precious family,
The comfort and the joy they give to me,
They fill my heart with gladness, joy and fun,
And do their best to keep me young.

Thank you for taking Brian to Heaven,
Out of his sickness and his pain,
Time pastes by as quickly as the rain,
One thing I am sure of is meeting Him again.

THE ANGELS

The little angels with their wings,
Sing melodies all day they sing,
They fly around in-groups of seven,
From here and there and back to heaven.

They help us creatures down below,
To make our lives so peaceful flow,
They are always at our beck and call,
And to help us rise up when we fall.

They guard and guide us on our way,
So it's up to us how we live our life,
They guard us from harm and danger,
Just like they surrounded Jesus in the manger.

THE GLORY OF GOD

When I look up at the stars in God's sky,
I thank God I give him glory and praise,
I contemplate His wonderful wisdom,
And give worship to His all-powerful ways.

He created all things out of nothing,
The sky the lakes and the mountains,
He created Man in His image and likeness,
His creation shone forth from His brightness.

He created animals so beautiful,
They each give Him glory in their own way.
The bees give us honey by the cupful,
All the birds praise Him in song night and day.

THE GOOD SHEPHERD

The Lord is the shepherd, who looks after His sheep,
Whether we are black or white we have no reason to weep,
He leads us to fresh meadows green,
So worry no more but swim in God's stream.

When we go through the dark tunnel of life,
He is there with His staff to help us to strive,
His light shines so bright it gladden the heart,
So be solders for Christ be really to march.

Never look back on the sad days again,
With Christ you are a winner from beginning to end,
So be happy and joyful on your pathway to heaven,
Sing songs with the angels on the old violin.

THE HOLY NIGHT

This is the holiest of nights,
Everything is silent and quite,
There is no place for Mary or Joseph to stay,
So Jesus is placed in a manger of hay.

The angels sing songs and give Him glory,
As everyone in heaven knows the whole story,
The sheep and the ox are asleep in the stable,
The birth of Jesus is no fable.

The shepherds see a star and are full of fright,
They do not understand so they pray for insight,
Angels appeared and said follow the star,
The king of kings is born not very far.

They enter the stable and prayed at the crib,
And praised God for this night and the graces He gives,
They are humble and poor and say why god choose us,
But God says the rich make too much of a fuss.

THE ROBIN

The robin red beast,
His Jesus Christ guest,
He sings and chirps and he is happy.
He hops and fly's until his wings are flappy,

The 1st Christmas night was ever so cold,
On came the robin bright and bold,
He flapped His wings to make the fire glow,
So that Mary and Joseph could go to and fro.

He flew up on the roof as the day was dawning,
He watched the shepherds kneeing and adoring,
He loved the three wise kings,
And in there presence to the Lord he sings.

THE SOURCE OF ALL LIFE

God is the source of all life,
Come you who are thirty for love,
He will fill your heart if you strife,
With blessings from heaven above.

Come to the throne of grace,
All who are lonely and sad,
God is the saviour of the human race,
He loves you so don't think you're bad,

Bathe in His Ocean of Mercy,
All who are suffering and sick,
He will heal all the burdens you carry,
All your ills will be healed very quick.

THE LIGHT OF CHRIST

Lets walk in His wonderful light,
Say goodbye to darkness and sin,
And read His gospel of truth,
Never again let His brightness go dim.

As we walk the pathways of life,
It is difficult sometimes to smile,
When sorrow pierces our hearts like a knife,
And we feel our lives as hard as a tile.

But with God at our side we are carried,
Over the rocks and the stones,
We then see light over the mountain,
And God's hands put a stop to our moans.

IN MY PRISON CELL

I look through the bars of my prison cell,
My story is painful and no one to tell,
All I see through the bars is just mud,
I am full of guilt and shame and feel such a dud.

The pain and the hurt I caused others,
My family my parents and brothers,
O' lord I feel broken and drained,
I am sorry for my life I have stained.

Lord Jesus come into my life,
 Please give me a new start,
So when I look through the bars I'll feel bright,
All then I will see will be stars.

THE TOUCH OF THE MASTER'S HAND

Touch our hearts so that we may love others,
Touch our tongues so that we might speak kindly
to our sisters and brothers,
Touch our minds to understand your ways,
Touch our feet to walk the path of life everyday.

Touch our ears to hear your words,
Touch our will to do the will of the Lord,
Touch our hands so that we will fill them with good deeds,
Touch our family so we will help one another when in need.

Touch our town every church and every steeple
Touch our country and its people,
Touch our hearts to give us affection,
Touch our lives when we need correction.

THE VIOLIN

If Jesus played the violin it would be harmonious,
It would never be out of tune,
There would be songs and dances in every room,
Every song and melody would be full of wisdom,
Telling people how to come into His kingdom.

All people would listen working in the meadows,
Then Jesus would reflect on them His shadows,
All the birds of the air would sing to His tune,
And earth would be no longer in the gloom.

It would be a new heaven and new earth,
With Jesus melodies and harmonies in the people would be a new birth,
Jesus is laughter and with Jesus the whole world has begun,
No more sadness because Jesus has turned our pain into gain.

THE WORD OF GOD

You word is a lamp to guide me,
It is a light on my path so I can see,
I will keep your commandments and laws,
Your ways and decrees have no flaws.

Your words are spirit and they are truth,
They have life and meaning and everyone they suit,
When we life by your word it brings joy and peace,
And thus our wonderful God is pleased.

The word of God is like a two-edge sword,
It cuts and is edgy it melts and moulds,
It bring joy to all those who are meek and mild,
It helps all creatures their God to find

VICTORY

In all things I have victory God is my deliver,
He is my strength and shield in all danger,
He protects me with His wings day and night,
I call on Him to defend me with all His might.

The Lord rewards me when I do what is right,
He dispels all darkness out of my life,
 When in trouble I call for help from the Lord,
He listens to my plea and I listen to His word,

I must keep alert and never give up,
Then overflowing will be my cup,
With graces and blessings reserved for a few,
What a wonderful God who aids us in all what we do.

WISDOM

Wisdom is the path to peace,
So start today and pray with your ease,
The wisdom of God is in all the gospels,
So from now on get hold of your missal.

Jesus is the way the truth and the life,
So give up your stubborn ways and try to be nice,
The Lord is near to all that call upon Him,
The Lord is gracious and full of compassion.

Praise the Lord with all your soul,
Praise Him morning noon and night,
Then our days will be no longer be dreary and dark,
But be filled with His beautiful presence so bright.